# The Gemini Book Everything You Should Know About Geminis

CRAFTED BY SKRIUWER

**Copyright © 2025 by Skriuwer.**

All rights reserved. No part of this book may be used or reproduced in any form whatsoever without written permission except in the case of brief quotations in critical articles or reviews.

At **Skriuwer**, we're more than just a team—we're a global community of people who love books. In Frisian, "Skriuwer" means "writer," and that's at the heart of what we do: creating and sharing books with readers worldwide. Wherever you are in the world, **Skriuwer** is here to inspire learning.

**Frisian** is one of the oldest languages in Europe, closely related to English and Dutch, and is spoken by about **500,000 people** in the province of **Friesland** (Fryslân), located in the northern Netherlands. It's the second official language of the Netherlands, but like many minority languages, Frisian faces the challenge of survival in a modern, globalized world.

We're using the money we earn to promote the Frisian language.

For more information, contact : **kontakt@skriuwer.com** (www.skriuwer.com)

# TABLE OF CONTENTS

## CHAPTER 1: UNDERSTANDING GEMINI BASICS

- How Gemini fits into the zodiac
- The link between curiosity, communication, and this sign
- Why Geminis adapt quickly in daily life

## CHAPTER 2: THE GEMINI SYMBOL AND BACKGROUND

- Origins of the "twins" image
- How myths shaped Gemini's core ideas
- The influence of Mercury on Gemini traits

## CHAPTER 3: SPECIAL TRAITS OF GEMINI PEOPLE

- Mental agility and quick thinking
- Social nature and love of learning
- Ways Geminis manage multiple interests

## CHAPTER 4: GEMINI AND COMMUNICATION

- Why Geminis are often natural communicators
- Challenges of switching topics too fast
- Tips for balancing talk and listening

## CHAPTER 5: CHALLENGES THAT GEMINI FACES

- Handling restlessness and unfinished projects
- Staying consistent without losing variety
- Overcoming stereotypes about being "scattered"

## CHAPTER 6: GEMINI IN FRIENDSHIPS

- *Bringing excitement to social circles*
- *Managing wide networks vs. deeper ties*
- *Suggestions for loyal, long-term Gemini bonds*

## CHAPTER 7: GEMINI IN THE FAMILY

- *Encouraging a Gemini's curiosity at home*
- *Navigating family roles and responsibilities*
- *Fostering understanding between different personalities*

## CHAPTER 8: GEMINI IN SCHOOL

- *Turning natural curiosity into academic success*
- *Avoiding boredom in repetitive lessons*
- *Using communication skills for group projects*

## CHAPTER 9: GEMINI EMOTIONS

- *Why Geminis often show feelings through talk*
- *Recognizing mood shifts and how to cope*
- *Deeper emotional expressions beneath the lively surface*

## CHAPTER 10: MAKING PLANS WITH GEMINI

- *Balancing spontaneity with practical details*
- *Adapting to last-minute changes gracefully*
- *Tips for coordinating group events with a Gemini*

## CHAPTER 11: GEMINI AND WORK LIFE

- *Career paths that suit Gemini's flexible mind*
- *Staying motivated when tasks become routine*
- *Positive ways Geminis thrive in team settings*

## CHAPTER 12: GEMINI HOBBIES AND FUN

- *Exploring multiple pastimes without feeling scattered*
- *Social hobbies vs. solo creative outlets*
- *Finding fulfilling ways to use spare time*

## CHAPTER 13: GEMINI AND HEALTH

- *Managing stress with a busy mind*
- *Physical activities that keep Geminis engaged*
- *Healthy routines and mindful eating tips*

## CHAPTER 14: GEMINI AND TECHNOLOGY

- *Why Geminis adapt quickly to new gadgets and apps*
- *Balancing screen time and real-world connections*
- *Using communication skills in digital communities*

## CHAPTER 15: GEMINI AND THEIR ENVIRONMENT

- *Creating stimulating yet calming personal spaces*
- *Adapting to city vs. rural life*
- *Making social areas and quiet corners at home*

## CHAPTER 16: COMMON MYTHS ABOUT GEMINI

- *Addressing labels like "two-faced" or "flaky"*
- *Clarifying why Geminis shift interests*
- *Proving sincerity through consistent actions*

## CHAPTER 17: GEMINI AND CLOSE RELATIONSHIPS

- *Building trust through open conversations*
- *Gemini traits in romantic, family, and friend bonds*
- *Balancing independence with emotional closeness*

## CHAPTER 18: FAMOUS GEMINIS

- *Notable figures who reflect Gemini qualities*
- *How adaptability shaped their achievements*
- *Diverse fields where Geminis stood out*

## CHAPTER 19: GEMINI THROUGH DIFFERENT AGES

- *How Gemini traits evolve from childhood to later life*
- *Key challenges and milestones in each stage*
- *Staying curious and adaptable across the years*

## CHAPTER 20: UNDERSTANDING GEMINI BETTER

- *Summarizing key Gemini traits and growth paths*
- *Practical tips for Geminis and their loved ones*
- *Integrating logic, curiosity, and empathy for lifelong growth*

# CHAPTER 1: UNDERSTANDING GEMINI BASICS

Gemini is one of the signs in the zodiac, which is a group of 12 signs people sometimes look at to learn about personality traits. Each sign has special qualities that set it apart from the others. To understand Gemini, it can help to start with the simplest facts. Gemini is often linked with the dates May 21 to June 20 (though sometimes the exact dates might change a little depending on how a person calculates the zodiac). People born between these dates are called Geminis.

Gemini belongs to a group of signs connected to air. In astrology, there are four elements: fire, earth, air, and water. Each element is known for a group of traits. Air signs are often tied to thinking, talking, and sharing thoughts. Some say that because Gemini is an air sign, it often involves quick thinking, curiosity, and a sense of excitement about learning new things. This idea may or may not feel right to everyone, because not all Geminis are alike, but many people find it helpful as a simple starting point.

Gemini's ruling planet is Mercury. In astrology, each sign is linked with a planet that might shape the sign's style. Mercury is often connected to how we talk, how we write, and how our minds work. Some people feel that Gemini is often good at chatting, picking up facts, and thinking about ideas in a fresh way. Others see Geminis as loving variety and liking many topics at once.

People sometimes call Gemini "the twins." That is because Gemini is often linked with the symbol of two figures who look alike. This might show the idea that Gemini can look at things in more than one way. Some see it as having two sides, while others see it as being open to many different paths. Because Gemini likes to explore ideas, they might change their mind or switch from one interest to another more quickly than some other signs.

Another basic idea is that Geminis like to learn. When you think of a Gemini, you might think of someone who asks lots of questions. You might also think of someone who likes sharing stories. It might be a person who is friends with many people, or who likes to talk about books, movies, or other things they enjoy. They might send messages to their friends or family and think of interesting topics to share.

It can be good to remember that not every Gemini is the same. People are also shaped by where they grew up, their family, their schooling, and many other factors. Astrology is just one way to understand personality traits. Still, many Geminis relate to the idea of being curious, social, and open to new topics.

Because Gemini is an air sign, it is sometimes paired with two other air signs: Libra and Aquarius. All three air signs are said to enjoy talking and thinking. But Gemini is often linked with being the one that loves bits of knowledge. They might like facts, trivia, and finding out about anything that catches their eye.

One of the simplest ways to see Gemini's nature is to look at how they deal with new things. A Gemini might get excited about a new book, game, or concept. Then, once they feel they know enough, they might move on to the next thing. This can make Gemini fun to be around, because they always have new things to share. It can also make them seem restless, because they might not stick with one hobby for a long time. They love to ask, "Why?" or "What does that mean?" or "How does that work?" They might be the ones who enjoy puzzles or guessing games.

Gemini is often seen as playful and lively. People who like astrology say that Geminis can be quick with jokes, come up with new ideas fast, and keep conversations flowing. If you think about how an air sign might behave, it makes sense. Air can move in many directions. Air can be calm or windy. In the same way, Gemini can change from being calm to excited. They might have a day when they are deep in thought, and another day when they are out meeting new people. They may have an open mind, ready to gather more information.

Another key point is that Geminis can handle more than one thing at a time. They might enjoy multitasking, such as talking on the phone while also writing a list or thinking about tomorrow's plans. This might seem like a lot, but many Geminis like having several things to do. They might get bored if they have to focus on only one thing for too long. They enjoy a change of pace to keep their minds active.

That said, Geminis sometimes are seen as inconsistent or "all over the place." This does not mean they do not care or cannot be reliable. It often means they are juggling many thoughts. One moment, they might want one thing, and later, they might choose something else. This can be fun because Geminis can be interesting to talk to. But it can also be confusing if you want them to be sure about a plan. Some Geminis work on being more steady when they need to be, while still keeping their love for new ideas.

Since Gemini is linked with Mercury, which is the planet of communication, Geminis often pay attention to words. They might like reading or writing. They might be good at picking up new languages or noticing small details in how people talk. If you know a Gemini, you might notice they can talk to many different kinds of people. They are often very adaptable in social settings. They might change how they speak depending on who they are with. For example, they might use simpler words when talking to a younger sibling but then switch to a more detailed style when talking to an adult.

For many Geminis, learning is fun. They might love to gather facts about many different things. Some people see Geminis as good at collecting random bits of knowledge. For example, they might know trivia about animals, sports, outer space, or music. They might remember jokes, quotes, or fun facts. They do not always go deep into these subjects, but they enjoy picking up bits and pieces.

When it comes to social life, Geminis are often seen as friendly. They can connect easily with others because they can talk about a wide range of things. They may get along with people who share their interests, and they can also adapt to different conversations. Sometimes, Geminis can seem scattered, but they often just have a fast mind that wants to do more than one thing at once. If you are a Gemini, you might feel that you love to chat with many different friends in one day, rather than spending all your time with just one friend. You might like to hop from one conversation to another.

Geminis can also be quick thinkers. They may like activities that allow them to use their minds. They might be good at word puzzles, guessing games, or spotting patterns. This is one reason many people think Geminis like to talk a lot, because they are always thinking. Still, everyone is different, and not all Geminis talk at the same pace or enjoy the same topics.

Another point about Gemini is that they can sometimes switch directions. This might mean they change their look, their interests, or even their plans. One week, they might like a certain band or movie, and the next, they might have moved on to something else. This can be fun because they always bring something new to a group of friends or family. But it can also be a source of confusion if people want them to be the same all the time. Geminis might need to work on balancing their love for variety with the need to stay steady at times.

A common thought about Gemini is that they can be good at explaining things. Because they are so used to talking and exploring different ideas, they might explain things in a way that others can understand. Some Geminis use this skill to help others learn. For example, they might make a good teacher or tutor, guiding friends through problems and offering advice. They might also know how to adjust their words so that they can share ideas with many different people.

Sometimes people wonder if Geminis are genuine, because Geminis can shift moods quickly. The truth is that many Geminis are quite honest, but they see different sides to the same issue. They might feel that there is more than one way to solve a problem or more than one way to think about a question. Because of this, a Gemini can be open to many points of view. They do not always lock themselves into a single mindset.

In friendships, Geminis might be the ones who suggest new activities. They might say, "Let's try this game," or "Let's go see something interesting." They bring energy and new ideas to the group. They might also surprise their friends by quickly changing their opinion if they learn something new. This flexible attitude can be helpful in some situations but might seem puzzling to people who like things to stay the same.

Because Geminis can think in different ways, they can be quite creative. They might be good at writing stories, telling jokes, making art, or coming up with games. They often have many ideas flowing through their heads. This can be exciting, but they might also get overwhelmed if they do not have a way to organize their thoughts. They might need to slow down sometimes and focus on what really matters to them.

You might be asking how all of this comes together. The main idea is that Gemini is a sign that loves to talk, think, share, and learn. It is also a sign that might like change and variety. If you are a Gemini, you might feel that you are a mix of many things. If you know a Gemini, you might see these traits appear in that person's life. Or you might see that some traits fit more than others.

People sometimes ask if Geminis are "two-faced," because of the twins symbol. This might come from the idea that Geminis can act differently in different settings. The truth is that many Geminis adapt to situations. They might seem silly in one moment and serious in the next. They might enjoy a wide range of moods. For them, it does not feel like being two-faced. It feels like being flexible and open to new experiences.

Gemini, as a word, comes from Latin and means "twins." The notion of twins shows the dual nature that people talk about with this sign. But if you look beyond that, it also shows how Geminis can bridge different worlds. They can bring people together by talking to different groups. They can spot connections between different ideas. They can be open to shifting viewpoints. This is why you might see Geminis playing the role of messenger in their circles, always passing on interesting news.

Finally, remember that while these ideas about Gemini can be helpful, they do not decide who you are as a person. Everyone has their own life experiences that shape them. Still, many people like to read about their sign because it can give a sense of shared traits. If you feel that Gemini basics match you, that might help you feel understood. If some points do not fit, that is okay too. Either way, you can use these traits in a positive way if you want.

# CHAPTER 2: THE GEMINI SYMBOL AND BACKGROUND

Gemini is often represented by the image of twins. In many old stories from different parts of the world, twins can show a link between two parts of life. In the world of astrology, the twins are sometimes tied to an old tale about Castor and Pollux from Greek myths. They were said to be twin brothers, though they had slightly different traits. One of them was said to be mortal (able to die), while the other was immortal (able to live forever). Their bond was strong, and they were placed in the sky as the constellation Gemini.

When we think about the Gemini symbol, we often picture two people standing or sitting next to each other. Sometimes, you might see a simplified symbol that looks like two columns joined at the top and bottom by horizontal lines. That shape is linked with Gemini in astrology charts. This twin idea suggests that Gemini can see both sides of a situation. It also suggests that Gemini might hold two ideas in the mind at once. Some people see it as a hint that Gemini can switch approaches when needed.

The history of astrology goes back many years to places like Babylonia, ancient Greece, and other cultures. People looked up at the stars and grouped them into constellations. They noticed that the sun seemed to pass through different groups of stars at certain times of the year. Gemini is one of these constellations in the sky, and it can be seen at certain times of the year if the sky is clear. Over time, people began to link each constellation with qualities that they believed shaped people's personalities. Gemini got its name from the Latin word meaning "twins."

The story of Castor and Pollux might help us see why Gemini is connected with traits like companionship and shared ideas. In the myth, the brothers were very close. They helped each other in difficult times. One version of the story says that when the mortal brother died, the immortal brother was so sad that he asked to share his immortal life so they could be together. The gods honored their request by placing them in the sky as the constellation Gemini. This might explain why people sometimes think of Geminis as being strong friends or partners. It also might explain why Gemini can be linked to loyalty in relationships, though they can sometimes seem easily distracted in day-to-day life.

In many star charts, you can find the constellation Gemini near Taurus and Cancer in the sky. The twins' stars are usually marked by two bright points called Castor and Pollux. This is one of the reasons each of those stars was named after one of the brothers in the myth. If you have a telescope or can look at a star map, you can spot Gemini more easily during certain months of the year (often in late fall or winter in the Northern Hemisphere).

The background of Gemini in astrology also involves the concept of Mercury, the ruling planet. Mercury, in Roman stories, was the messenger god. He moved quickly and carried messages from place to place. In Greek stories, the messenger god was Hermes, who also wore winged sandals. The idea is that Mercury is all about quick thinking, travel, and communication. Gemini, being ruled by Mercury, might share these traits. That is why people think of Geminis as talkative, mentally quick, and ready to learn. In old times, people believed that the planet Mercury had a special influence on people born when the sun was in Gemini. Today, even if someone does not believe in the power of the planets, they can still enjoy the mythic stories that give the zodiac signs a special flavor.

Thinking about the symbol of twins, we can see how it shapes the idea of Gemini in many ways. For example, the twins might mean having a double nature. Some people say this could show in day-to-day behavior: a Gemini might be happy and excited one moment and quiet and thoughtful the next. Or it might mean that a Gemini likes to look at problems from two or more angles. They are not limited to just one point of view. This can be good because it means Geminis can be flexible. But it might also cause them to struggle with making decisions if they see too many possibilities.

The Gemini background also includes the sense of being open to new knowledge and eager to share it. Twins can represent a back-and-forth flow. Imagine two people who like to talk with each other, passing ideas from one mind to another. This can be how Geminis interact with the world. They collect facts and information, and then they share them with others. The symbol of twins can stand for the concept of connection—connecting people to each other, connecting ideas, or connecting different parts of life.

Because Gemini is part of the zodiac cycle, each sign has a season. Gemini season is roughly from late May to late June. During this time, spring is moving toward summer in the Northern Hemisphere. For many people, this season feels fresh, active, and buzzing with life. The days grow longer, and the weather (in many places) becomes warmer. Some people link Gemini's lively energy to the feeling of the world opening up during this time of year. Of course, in the Southern Hemisphere, the seasons are flipped, but the zodiac signs remain the same months. Still, the general idea is that Gemini's time is a period of change and movement.

Looking at the background of Gemini also helps us see why many Geminis might feel restless if they do not have something new to learn or talk about. The symbol of twins can be seen as a reminder that Geminis thrive on exchange. They do not want to stay in one spot for too long. They often like to move around, not just physically but mentally. They might jump from talking about a cool new animal they learned about to sharing a story about a friend's interesting hobby. This can keep life exciting and fresh.

Another part of Gemini's background is that it is a "mutable" sign. In astrology, each sign is also classified as cardinal, fixed, or mutable. Mutable signs (Gemini, Virgo, Sagittarius, Pisces) are said to be adaptable, able to see many possibilities, and sometimes less stable than the fixed signs. This adds another layer to how we understand Gemini. The twins might shift between different states of mind, showing that Geminis can adapt to different situations or people. They might not cling to one routine as much as some other signs do.

It can also help to know that Gemini's symbol and background speak to how people born in this sign might behave in group settings. Twins suggest sharing. A group of friends with a Gemini in it might find that the Gemini is the connector, the one who brings different groups together or who stays in touch with friends from different circles. This can be helpful if you want to make a bigger group and have fun. Gemini might also be the one who changes plans often, which can be interesting or frustrating depending on what others prefer.

The twin symbol can also be seen in how Geminis often have a strong link between their mind and how they express themselves. They might feel that their thoughts move at a quick speed, and they need to speak or write to let them out. This could lead to creative projects, journaling, or any activity that lets them share what is on their mind. Sometimes, Geminis might even surprise themselves with how much they want to talk about a subject. It is as if the twin symbol within them is always saying, "But there is more!" or "What if we look at it another way?" or "Let's keep the conversation going."

People who study astrology in depth look at a lot more than just the sun sign. They look at the entire birth chart, which includes the moon sign, rising sign, and the positions of other planets. But for a simple look at Gemini, focusing on the twin symbol, Mercury's influence, and the air element is enough to give a child-friendly overview.

In different cultures, the Gemini symbol might have different stories attached. Some see the twins as a symbol of close friendship. Others might tie it to tales of trickster spirits that can change form. But the common thread is that the twins show duality—two sides, two approaches, and a sense of motion between them. In astrology, this means that Gemini can be quick-witted, curious, and versatile.

Even the name "Gemini" links us to its meaning. In Latin, "gemini" simply means "twins." Many languages have a similar word that comes from the same root. Over time, this name stayed with the constellation and the zodiac sign. When someone says they are a Gemini, they are basically saying they are born under the sign of the twins. This can feel special to someone who likes the idea of being linked to a mythic story about strong bonds and shared adventures.

Another interesting fact is that in some older writings, Gemini was also associated with siblings or sibling-like friendships. This might come from the idea that the sign of the twins can point to close connections between people who can almost read each other's minds. Geminis might often have a sibling-like bond with their close friends, finishing each other's sentences or laughing at the same jokes. In a way, this might be the background energy of the sign at play.

When we look at the background of the Gemini symbol, it can remind us that astrology is not just about personal traits. It is also about stories in the stars, old myths, and the ways humans have tried to make sense of life by looking up at the night sky. Whether or not someone believes in astrology as truth, there is value in looking at the myths and symbols that have come down through history. They can tell us something about how people long ago thought about friendship, loyalty, curiosity, and the power of sharing ideas.

It is also interesting to note how the Gemini symbol is one of the few zodiac symbols that clearly shows two people. Some other signs are animals or objects. Gemini, on the other hand, highlights the human side, reflecting how Geminis can be very people-oriented. They like to talk, laugh, and share experiences. This might be why many people think of Geminis as being more focused on the human aspects of life than on quiet solitude.

As we understand the Gemini symbol and background, it is helpful to keep an open mind about the ways these ideas show up in real life. Astrology stories might be fun, but each Gemini has their own personality. Some Geminis might be shy. Others might be very outgoing. Still, the symbol of the twins reminds us that Gemini often involves thinking, connecting, and a certain spark of mental curiosity.

Let's gather the main points about the Gemini symbol and background:

**Twins Image**: Gemini is linked to twins, sometimes connected to Castor and Pollux from Greek myths. This stands for close bonds, two sides, and the idea of companionship or duality.

**Constellation**: In the night sky, Gemini is a constellation with two bright stars named after Castor and Pollux. It is part of the circle of zodiac constellations.

**Latin Meaning**: The word "Gemini" comes from Latin, meaning "twins." This points directly to the sign's main symbol.

**Myth and History**: Astrological ideas about Gemini go back a long time. Stories explain how the twins ended up in the sky. This has shaped how people think about Gemini's traits.

**Planet Mercury**: Gemini is ruled by Mercury, the messenger planet, which is tied to talking, writing, learning, and quick movement. This adds to the image of Gemini as a thinking and talking sign.

**Air Element**: Being an air sign connects Gemini with ideas, thoughts, and exchanges. This can explain why Geminis are known for curiosity and sharing information.

**Mutable Sign**: Gemini is also known as a mutable sign, meaning it is flexible and able to adapt. The twin symbol can show two sides or two paths Gemini might take.

**Season**: Gemini season is around late May to late June, a time that can feel energetic and active. This matches Gemini's lively spirit.

**Connection to People**: The twin symbol also highlights that Geminis might have a strong desire to talk and bond with others, often building many friendships.

**Changing Moods**: The twin image can also hint at quick changes in mood or focus. This is not always bad—it can mean Gemini can handle change well.

**Sibling-Like Bond**: The background story sometimes points to strong friendships or sibling-like bonds, showing loyalty and shared interests.

**Mythic Value**: Even if someone is not interested in astrology, the stories about the twins can be a way to learn about ancient myths and how people have viewed the stars.


That is how the Gemini symbol and background fit together. It gives us a sense of why Gemini is represented by twins, how that idea came from old myths, and why people born under this sign often enjoy talking, learning, and connecting with others. Some see Gemini as a sign that can easily move from one interest to another, shining a light on many topics. They are the people who might have friends from different walks of life, and they can slip in and out of different roles. The twins might also remind us that Gemini can have both a light, playful side and a deeper, more thoughtful side.

This background sets the stage for understanding Gemini as a whole. It explains a big part of why Gemini is seen as a sign of conversation, mental activity, and curiosity. In later chapters, we will look more closely at how these traits show up in everyday life, including how Geminis act in friendships, school, family, and more. But for now, this deep look at the Gemini symbol—twins—and the stories linked to it can help us see why people often label Gemini as the sign of the "twofold mind" or the sign of dual perspectives.

While it might sound strange to have a zodiac sign that shows two people rather than one creature or object, it actually fits quite well with Gemini's trait of variety and flexibility. Geminis might love the idea that their sign is linked to the concept of having more than one viewpoint. They might also enjoy the idea that part of their background comes from a caring story about brothers who wanted to stay together forever. These ideas can help Geminis see their sign as one that values friendship, learning, and connecting.

Because the Gemini symbol is so recognizable, many Geminis feel a sense of pride in having the twins as their sign. They might draw pictures of the twins, or wear jewelry with the Gemini glyph (the two columns), or mention the story of Castor and Pollux to explain part of their personality. Whether or not someone believes fully in astrology, it can be fun to learn about these myths and symbols. The stories are a big part of human history, and they can bring people together. After all, Gemini is about conversation and making connections. Sharing these tales can spark interesting chats.

In conclusion, the Gemini symbol and background give us an important framework for everything else that will come later in this book. By knowing that Gemini is represented by twins with a rich myth behind them, that it is ruled by Mercury, and that it belongs to the air element, we can see how

Gemini got its traits. Geminis might show quick-thinking, a love for conversation, an adaptable nature, and a wish to keep learning. The twins highlight the idea that Gemini can handle multiple perspectives and might even seem to shift from one mood to another.

With these details in mind, we will move on to more specific parts of Gemini life in the next chapters. We will look at special traits of Gemini people, their approach to talking, the challenges they might face, and much more. All of that rests on the foundation built by the Gemini symbol, which has stood for curiosity and flexibility for a very long time.

# CHAPTER 3: SPECIAL TRAITS OF GEMINI PEOPLE

Geminis are often linked with a range of interesting traits that shape how they behave from day to day. While not every Gemini is the same, many share certain habits or preferences that make them stand out. In this chapter, we will look at some of these traits and see why people often think Geminis have a special spark. We will keep the language clear and easy to follow, so everyone can understand.

## A Thirst for Knowledge

One of the most well-known traits of many Geminis is that they like to learn. They might have a shelf full of books, or they might follow a lot of different topics on the internet. When a Gemini finds a new subject that interests them, they can be very excited about it. This excitement might last for a while, or it might switch to something else if they find something even more appealing.

This eagerness to know things can show up in small ways, too. For example, a Gemini might enjoy reading fun facts on snack wrappers, or they might watch many short videos online about science or history. They rarely get bored because there is always something out there that sparks their mind. It could be a new word they discovered or a strange fact about animals. In short, Geminis often have minds that are ready to gather information at all times.

## Adaptability

Geminis often adjust to new situations more easily than some other signs. They might be happy in a quiet place, reading or writing, but they can also go to a busy event and talk to everyone in the room. This ability to adapt means they rarely feel stuck in any situation.

For instance, if a Gemini's teacher changes the seating chart at school, they might not be too upset. Instead, they might see it as a chance to meet new classmates or get a fresh perspective in the classroom. If their family moves to a new city, they might try to learn all about the new location right away. Some Geminis even look forward to big changes because it gives them something new to figure out.

It is worth noting that adaptability can be a strength, but it can also come with challenges. Sometimes, switching from one situation to another can be tiring. Still, many Geminis seem to handle it well, because they like variety and do not mind surprises.

## Quick Thinking

Another special trait of many Gemini people is that they can think fast. Their minds can jump from one thought to another in a short time. This quick thinking might help them come up with ideas or clever answers. They can be the friend who instantly has a suggestion about where to go for fun, or who can solve a small puzzle in seconds.

In a classroom setting, a Gemini might speak up first if the teacher asks a question. Their mind runs quickly, so they might figure out the answer before others do. Of course, this does not mean they always have the correct answer. But they are often quick to try. At the same time, their speed can lead to some mistakes if they do not slow down and think things through carefully. As a result, Geminis sometimes benefit from practicing patience. Yet, this quickness can be exciting to watch and is part of what makes them stand out.

## Creative Flair

Because Geminis pick up new ideas so easily, they often have a creative side. Their creativity might show up in writing, drawing, music, or even making up games to play with friends. They might enjoy telling funny stories or making clever jokes. They tend to absorb bits of inspiration from many places—a book they read, a show they watched, or a conversation they overheard.

Geminis do not always stick to one creative hobby for long. They might try painting one month and then switch to writing short poems the next. This can be confusing for people around them, who might wonder why the Gemini is not focusing on just one art form. However, for the Gemini, it feels natural to try new things. Their curiosity leads them to see what each form of art or expression is like.

Some Geminis might combine ideas in unique ways. They can take a concept from one topic and link it with a completely different topic, coming up with something fresh. This means they can be good at brainstorming in school or at work. People often appreciate a Gemini's ability to add new ideas to a project, even if those ideas might need polishing later.

## Sense of Humor

Many Geminis love jokes and humor. They often see the funny side of a situation, which helps lighten the mood. A Gemini might share something amusing they read earlier or come up with a silly pun on the spot. They might also enjoy playing pranks on friends, though hopefully in a harmless way.

Because they are quick thinkers, Geminis can respond with funny one-liners during conversations. They might also be the type who giggles at random moments, remembering a clever thought from earlier in the day. Their humor can sometimes be playful teasing, but most Geminis do not mean to hurt anyone's feelings. They simply like to keep things light and entertaining.

Their sense of humor can break tension in a group setting. If everyone is nervous, a Gemini might share a funny thought or story to help people relax. This makes them fun to have around, especially during stressful events. However, they should also learn when to be serious, because some situations call for a calmer tone. Finding that balance helps Geminis get along with lots of different people.

## Need for Variety

Geminis often crave new experiences. This ties in with their adaptability and quick thinking. If they do the same activity repeatedly, they can become restless. They might switch to a new hobby, or they might want to rearrange their schedule. This need for variety can keep life interesting, but it can also mean they sometimes struggle with long-term tasks that require steady focus.

For example, if a Gemini is involved in a big project that goes on for months, they might get bored halfway through if there is nothing new happening. They might start to wish they could try something else. To manage this, Geminis may look for ways to keep their tasks fresh, such as breaking them into smaller steps or adding fun details.

In friendships, their need for variety might mean that Geminis want to hang out with different groups of people. They might not always stick to just one circle of friends. This can help them connect with many personalities and share stories from one group to another. Still, it can be helpful for Geminis to remember that some friends might want more steady time with them. Learning to balance their desire for variety with loyalty can be a helpful skill.

## Friendly Nature

While not every single Gemini is outgoing, many of them enjoy talking to others and forming friendships. They can be quite open-minded, which makes them good at meeting people from different backgrounds. Because Geminis are often curious, they ask questions about people's interests or life experiences. This can make others feel valued and seen.

Geminis also know how to adjust their communication style to different social settings. They might be lively and fun in one context, and more thoughtful or quiet in a setting that requires it. This helps them fit in, but it can also cause confusion if someone expects them to act the same way all the time. In general, though, people often appreciate that Geminis can make conversation flow easily. If there is a lull, a Gemini might think of a new topic to keep things going.

## Being Good with Words

One reason Geminis are often seen as friendly is that they are skilled with words. They might talk a lot, but they also tend to do it in a way that is interesting. They might use humor, interesting facts, or quick comebacks. Some Geminis even enjoy public speaking or debate because they can gather information and then present it in a lively way.

Their skill with words can also show up in writing. Some Geminis enjoy writing stories, poems, or articles. They might keep a journal or create stories for fun. Because they have so many ideas, they often have a lot to say. However, they might not always finish every writing project they start, especially if a new idea comes along. Still, when a Gemini does stick with a writing goal, they can produce something quite inventive, because their mind is bursting with different perspectives.

Being good with words can also mean Geminis are good at explaining things to others. They might break down a complex idea into smaller parts so that friends or family can understand it. They may use examples or simple language to make something clear. This can be helpful in group projects, tutoring, or just everyday life when someone is confused about a topic.

## Possible Struggles with Consistency

One thing that can challenge Geminis is consistency. Because their minds move quickly, they might switch from one hobby to another or even change their opinions frequently. Sometimes, they sign up for many clubs, classes, or tasks, only to find that they do not have enough time or energy to handle them all. This can leave them feeling scattered or overwhelmed.

A Gemini might also start a creative hobby with great excitement but drop it after a few weeks once the novelty wears off. The same can happen with exercise routines or other daily habits. Maintaining consistency can be tough when there are so many new things to try. To work on this, some Geminis find it helpful to keep a planner or a schedule that reminds them of their responsibilities.

It can also help if they choose a few tasks that really matter to them. Rather than jumping into many new activities at once, they might decide on one or two that feel most important. This approach can help them stick to a plan and still leave room for exploring fresh ideas.

## Observant Eye

Geminis are often good at noticing small details. They might spot a subtle change in someone's mood or realize that something in the room has been moved. Their quick mind picks up on these details, and they might use them in conversation. For instance, they might say, "You seem a bit quieter today," or "Did you change your hairstyle?" This can make others feel like the Gemini is paying attention.

Being observant can help a Gemini in problem-solving, too. They might catch a hint or clue that others miss. In a game that requires noticing patterns, a Gemini might excel. However, this observant nature can also lead them to become easily distracted. They might notice so many small things around them that they lose focus on the main task. Learning how to use their observant eye without losing focus is something many Geminis work on.

## Ability to Shift Between Moods

Because Geminis can see many sides of a situation, they might shift their mood or viewpoint faster than some other signs. One moment, they might be excited about a plan, and the next moment, they might feel unsure if it is the right idea. This can be puzzling to people around them who do not change their minds as quickly.

Sometimes, Geminis just need time to think about different possibilities. They might talk with friends or family to get input. They might compare pros and cons or even role-play different outcomes in their head. It can be helpful if their loved ones are patient with this process. Once a Gemini decides on a path, they can be quite enthusiastic, but they might go through several "try-outs" of different ideas before settling on one.

## Balancing the Twin Sides

Because Gemini is linked with the idea of twins, there is often talk about two sides within them. While this does not mean they are two different people, it can mean they have varied parts to their personality. One side might be very outgoing, the other side might be thoughtful and calm. One side might be serious about a topic, and the other side might see the amusing angle of the same topic.

This can lead to internal conflicts, where a Gemini wonders which side to follow. For instance, should they continue with a responsible plan, or should they do something more fun and spontaneous? These internal debates can be tough, but they also let Geminis see a bigger picture. They often learn to combine these sides in a way that helps them adapt to life's changes.

## Warm-Hearted but Sometimes Distant

A Gemini can be very warm and kind, checking in on friends and asking how they are doing. At the same time, they might distance themselves if they feel bored or if another topic pulls them away. This can happen in friendships, where a Gemini is very active for a while, then becomes busy with new interests and is less available.

It is not that they care any less; it is just that their attention might get pulled in many directions. Learning to show steadiness in their relationships can be important. Loved ones might appreciate a message or phone call from time to time, even if the Gemini is exploring new activities. Some Geminis set reminders to stay in touch with people, which can help them show they still care.

## Using Logic and Curiosity Together

Geminis often combine logical thinking with a hungry mind. They might break down a situation step by step, using logic to see how it works. At the same time, they might ask all sorts of questions about it. For example, if they are learning about computers, they might take them apart in their mind: "How does this part fit with that one? Why does it work this way?" Then they might search for answers in books or online.

This blend of logic and curiosity can make them good at puzzles or tasks that require problem-solving. They enjoy a riddle or mystery that makes them think. If a friend has a problem, a Gemini might offer both logical advice and a few side comments that spark new ideas. However, because they are so open to new information, they might also get sidetracked. They may start looking into the history of computers when they only meant to solve a small glitch.

## Tendency to Talk Through Problems

When a Gemini faces a problem, they might talk about it with many people. They could share their thoughts with a friend, a family member, or even someone online. Talking helps them organize their ideas. It can be comforting for them to speak openly. In fact, some Geminis say they do their best thinking when they can say the words out loud, even if they are just talking to themselves in a private space.

This can be good because it helps them gain multiple views and can lead them to find a better solution. On the other hand, some people might find it surprising that the Gemini is talking about the same problem again and again. Geminis should remember that not everyone wants to analyze an issue in such detail. Still, for the Gemini, it can be a natural process that helps them figure out what they truly think or feel.

## Love for Sharing Random Facts

Because Geminis pick up information from many sources, they often remember random bits of trivia. They might tell you something about a strange event in history or share a fact about how a certain food is made. These random facts might pop up during conversations, adding color to the discussion. Some friends find this trait fascinating, while others might roll their eyes if they prefer to stick to the main topic.

For Geminis, sharing random facts is not just about showing off knowledge. It is also a way to connect and keep the conversation fresh. They enjoy seeing people react to new pieces of information. Sometimes, their facts can even help solve a small problem, like when someone wonders about a certain detail and the Gemini happens to know the answer.

## Being Flexible in Plans

Another special Gemini trait is flexibility in making plans. If they decided to do one activity but then heard of something else more interesting, they might switch. This can be both helpful and challenging. On one hand, they are never stuck doing something they no longer enjoy. On the other hand, it can be frustrating for friends who want a set plan.

For instance, if a Gemini friend said they would watch a movie with you on Saturday, but on Friday they found out about a fun event, they might ask you to change your plans. They are not trying to be rude; they just genuinely believe the new activity might be more exciting for both of you. However, if friends value routine, they might feel let down. Striking a balance can help a Gemini keep their friendships strong while still keeping life interesting.

## A Childlike Wonder

Geminis sometimes keep a sense of wonder about the world, even as they grow older. They might still be amazed by simple things, like a cool rock they found or a bright rainbow after a storm. Their mind is always noticing fresh details, and they can get excited about things that other people might pass by without a second thought.

This childlike sense of wonder can make them fun to be around. They might point out a tiny bug that looks unique or share a random observation about clouds in the sky. This excitement can be contagious, reminding others to find interest in the little things around them. However, it also means Geminis might be easily distracted by new things that catch their eye. They should be mindful of when they need to focus on a task instead of drifting away to look at something else.

## Ability to Handle Several Conversations

Since Geminis are good at talking, they might handle more than one conversation at once. For example, they might text a friend while also chatting with a family member in the same room. This can be impressive, but it also risks splitting their attention. Sometimes, they might mix up details or accidentally ignore one person while paying attention to another.

Still, this multi-conversation skill can help them manage group chats or social media. They might keep track of multiple threads and respond to each in a timely way. However, it is wise for Geminis to remember that focusing on one conversation at a time can show respect to the person they are with. Balancing their natural interest in many things with the need to be present in the moment is an important lesson.

## Enthusiasm for Ideas

One of the most charming Gemini traits is pure enthusiasm for ideas of all kinds. Whether it is a new style of music, a funny joke, a puzzle, or a big plan for the future, Geminis can light up when they hear something that sparks their interest. This enthusiasm can spread to the people around them, helping everyone get excited.

They might dream up plans for a cool project, like starting a comic club or coming up with a new recipe. They often have a "Why not?" attitude. If an idea sounds interesting, they are willing to consider it. The downside is that they might collect so many ideas that they never act on half of them. Yet, many Geminis would say that it is better to have too many ideas than too few.

## Learning Through Conversation

Geminis gather information not just from books and the internet but also from chatting with others. They might have deep talks with a grandparent about how things were years ago, or they might listen closely to a friend who has a different view on something. Because Geminis love to ask questions, they can learn a lot this way.

Sometimes, people might feel surprised by how much detail a Gemini remembers. But for the Gemini, it can be natural to store bits of information from every person they speak to. They might remember a random comment about someone's favorite food and bring it up later if it becomes relevant. This approach to learning can be both social and educational at the same time.

## Handling Stress

Like anyone, Geminis face stress in different parts of life. Their flexible nature might help them deal with sudden changes, but at times, the sheer number of thoughts in their head can feel overwhelming. If a Gemini has too many tasks going on, they might become restless or anxious. They might even forget important items on their to-do list because their mind is juggling so many things.

**To handle stress better, a Gemini might**:

- Write down tasks so they do not forget.
- Talk to a close friend or family member about their worries.
- Take short breaks to clear their mind.
- Find a fun outlet, like drawing or a word puzzle, to calm down.

Because they often enjoy variety, it might help them to rotate through a few relaxation methods. For example, they could try listening to soothing music one day and taking a nature walk the next. As long as they remember to keep track of important responsibilities, these methods can keep stress in check.

## Openness to New Perspectives

Geminis tend to welcome new perspectives. They might talk to someone who disagrees with them on a topic and still come away feeling they learned something. This does not mean a Gemini always changes their mind, but they are less likely to shut someone down right away. They might ask questions to understand why the other person thinks that way.

This openness can help them grow. They might gather insights from different people and then form an opinion that includes bits of each side. Sometimes, they end up with a view that is in the middle, or they might discover a point they had never considered before. However, a Gemini should be mindful not to let too many other opinions drown out their own sense of self. They can listen to many views and still keep their own core values.

## Magnetic Charisma

Because of their bright ideas and playful spirit, many Geminis have a certain charisma. They might not be the loudest person in the room, but they often draw attention through jokes, interesting facts, or warm smiles. People might say that a Gemini has a special spark that makes them appealing to talk to. They seem "alive" in a way that catches interest.

This does not mean every Gemini is the same kind of charismatic. Some might have a quieter appeal, attracting others by being a thoughtful listener. But in general, Geminis tend to have something about them that makes people want to engage in conversation. As long as the Gemini remains respectful and kind, this trait can open doors in both personal and professional situations.

## Conclusion

Geminis often stand out for their mental quickness, love of new information, and flexible approach to life. They can be fun, sociable, and always ready to discuss something. They might switch gears more often than others do, but this is part of their charm. They bring an energy that can brighten a room and spark laughter or interesting debates. It is important for them to remember that consistency can help them complete tasks and keep relationships strong.

# CHAPTER 4: GEMINI AND COMMUNICATION

Communication is often called the heart of what makes Geminis shine. Because many Geminis have a knack for words, they tend to do well in conversations, whether they are chatting with friends, writing messages, or speaking in front of a group. In this chapter, we will look at how Geminis communicate in different parts of life, from casual talks to more serious discussions. We will also talk about challenges they might face and ways they can improve.

## Love of Conversation

Geminis usually enjoy talking, plain and simple. They might be the ones asking questions, telling stories, or sharing interesting facts. In a group of friends, a Gemini can keep the conversation moving. If the chatter starts to slow down, they might ask, "Hey, did anyone see that weird article about sharks?" or "I heard an amusing story about my neighbor's cat." These sudden topic shifts can keep people on their toes.

One reason Geminis love to talk is that they have a lot going on in their minds. They pick up bits of information wherever they go—at school, online, or just from daily life—and they want to share what they have learned. For them, conversation is not only a way to be social; it is also a way to process ideas. By speaking about something, they make sense of it for themselves.

## Asking Lots of Questions

Because Geminis tend to be curious, they are often the ones in the group asking many questions. This might happen in school when they want more details from the teacher, or in a social setting when they want to learn about someone's background or hobbies. Some people enjoy being asked questions because it shows genuine interest. Others might feel a bit overwhelmed if the questions come too quickly.

A Gemini who learns how to pace their questions can become a wonderful conversationalist. They give others the feeling of being listened to and cared about. But it is good for a Gemini to notice if someone seems uncomfortable or tired of talking. In those cases, a little break or a simpler approach can help the conversation stay balanced.

## Changing Topics Quickly

One challenge for Geminis is that they might switch topics faster than other people can follow. Their minds move quickly, and they might think, "We already spent too long on that subject. Let's talk about something else." While this can be fun and exciting, it can also cause confusion. If the group is still interested in the first topic, they might feel left behind when the Gemini jumps to a new one.

To help with this, a Gemini can remind themselves to check if the group is ready to shift topics. They can say, "Does anyone else have thoughts on this before we move on?" This small step can keep everyone on the same page. It can also help the Gemini slow down and listen more closely to what others have to say.

## Strong Skills in Writing

Many Geminis are not just good at talking; they can also be skilled at writing. They might write detailed emails or texts that are both clear and friendly. They might have a flair for creative writing, such as short stories or poems. Their ability to find the right words can help them share information or feelings in an effective way.

When writing, a Gemini might enjoy using humor or adding interesting facts. They might also like to experiment with different writing styles. For example, they could try writing in a diary format one day and a fiction format the next. Because they love variety, they are not afraid to test new ways of expressing themselves. The only risk is that they might start a writing project and not finish it if they lose interest or move on to another idea. However, when a Gemini is truly motivated, they can produce writing that stands out.

## Handling Public Speaking

Some Geminis find that speaking in front of a group comes naturally. Their comfort with words can make it easier for them to stand up and share ideas. They might join clubs or events that let them present or perform. At the same time, not every Gemini is a natural extrovert. Some Geminis prefer smaller group talks. Yet even the quieter Geminis might surprise people with how well they speak once they feel comfortable.

Public speaking allows Geminis to channel their quick thinking. They can adapt to questions or comments as they come. If someone in the audience asks something unexpected, the Gemini might come up with a clever answer on the spot. This skill can help them in school presentations or even later in life, such as in work meetings or community events.

## Social Media and Texting

Communication for Geminis often extends into social media and texting. Because they like to connect with lots of people, they might have accounts on multiple platforms and talk to many friends throughout the day. They might enjoy sending quick, witty messages or interesting links. They may also post about random facts or short thoughts that cross their mind.

The upside is that Geminis can keep their relationships active, even from a distance. However, they should be careful not to spread themselves too thin. If a Gemini is talking to ten people at once, they might struggle to give each person the attention they deserve. Also, because Geminis can sometimes get bored easily, they might spend too much time scrolling and not enough time doing other important tasks. Finding a balance between online chatting and real-life responsibilities can be crucial.

## Listening vs. Talking

One area where Geminis can grow is balancing how much they talk with how much they listen. Because they have so much to say, they might accidentally dominate a conversation. In some cases, people might feel they cannot get a word in. A Gemini might notice that they have been talking for a while and then remember to ask, "What do you think?" or "How about you?"

Developing strong listening skills is important for any good communicator. Geminis who learn to pause and hear others' viewpoints can form deeper connections. They might discover that others also have interesting facts or stories to share. Listening can also give Geminis new ideas, which they love to gather. So, if a Gemini wants to be a great communicator, they should keep track of how often they speak compared to how often they listen.

## Handling Conflict

When conflicts happen, Geminis might try to talk their way through them. They might offer many ideas for solving the issue or try to explain their side in detail. Their quick mind helps them think of many possible solutions. However, in emotional arguments, too much talking might come across as not wanting to listen to the other person.

Geminis can benefit from taking a moment to breathe and let the other person speak. They can say, "I want to understand your point of view." Then, they can share their own thoughts in a calm way. Because they are adaptable, Geminis can be good at finding a middle ground. But they need to remember that conflicts are not just about logic; they often involve feelings, too.

## Enjoyment of Group Discussions

Group discussions are often a place where Geminis can shine. They can bring up points that nobody else thought about. They might also connect different ideas brought up by various group members. For example, if one person suggests a plan and another person shares a problem with it, the Gemini might see a compromise that blends both ideas.

In these discussions, a Gemini's job can be like that of a bridge, linking different points of view. They might say, "I see what you're saying, and I also understand their idea. What if we try something in between?" People often appreciate this ability. Still, Geminis should be careful not to jump too quickly to the next topic before everyone has finished talking about the first one. Doing so could confuse the group or leave some thoughts unheard.

## Playful Banter

Many Geminis enjoy playful banter—light teasing or back-and-forth jokes with friends. They might send funny texts, come up with puns, or give friends silly nicknames. This banter can make friendships lively and entertaining. However, they should watch out for when teasing might go too far. Some people are more sensitive, and a joke that seems harmless to the Gemini might sting someone else.

When a Gemini notices that someone is not laughing along, they can slow down and apologize or clarify that they meant no harm. Because they are often skilled at reading people's expressions, they can usually sense if the mood changes. Pausing to make sure everyone is okay can help keep the playful banter fun for all.

## Switching Between Serious and Silly Tones

Geminis are known for switching quickly from a serious tone to a silly one. In conversation, they might be talking about an important issue one moment and crack a joke the next. Sometimes, this can ease tension and show that they are not stuck in one mode. Other times, it might seem disrespectful if the subject is very serious. Striking the right balance is key.

For example, if a friend is talking about something sad, it might be best for the Gemini to stay sympathetic and supportive rather than trying to lighten the mood immediately. Once the moment feels right, a small joke or upbeat comment can help, but timing is everything. Geminis who pay attention to the signals others give off usually figure out when humor is welcome and when it is not.

## Body Language and Gestures

When Geminis speak, they often use facial expressions and gestures to get their points across. They might use their hands while talking or make silly faces when telling a funny story. This adds liveliness to their communication style. Some Geminis are so expressive that even if you do not understand their language, you might sense what they are feeling from their tone and body movements.

Body language can help Geminis make a stronger connection. For instance, leaning in a bit when someone else is talking shows interest. Nodding can let others know you are listening. At the same time, they should watch out for too much movement, which might distract people. Finding a comfortable balance lets a Gemini's expressions add to their words without overwhelming others.

## Digital Communication Challenges

While Geminis may be skilled at messaging and posting online, the digital world also has pitfalls. Because they move from topic to topic so easily, they might sign up for multiple group chats or platforms. This can result in a flood of notifications. If a Gemini tries to keep up with all of them, they might never have time to focus on offline tasks.

Also, in texting or online forums, tone can be hard to read. A Gemini who loves playful sarcasm might accidentally offend someone if the other person cannot hear the friendly tone of voice. To avoid misunderstandings, Geminis can add a friendly emoji or clarify that they are just kidding. They can also remember that not everyone likes jokes in every context. Adjusting to different online spaces can improve their digital interactions.

## Communicating New Ideas

Geminis are often bursting with new ideas, and they love to share them. Whether it is a suggestion for a class project or a fun activity for the weekend, they want to talk it through. To make sure others understand and accept their ideas, they can break them down into smaller steps. If they throw out a huge, complicated plan all at once, people might feel overwhelmed.

For instance, if a Gemini has an idea for a school event, they could start by explaining the main goal. Then, they could list the steps needed to make it happen. They could invite feedback from others, which shows that they respect different opinions. This approach often leads to a better outcome than just declaring an idea and moving on to something else before others can respond.

## Teaching and Explaining

Because Geminis are good at gathering information, they can be great at explaining things to others. They might be the friend who helps someone understand a math problem, or who shows a younger sibling how to bake cookies. Their strength lies in breaking down details into simpler chunks. This can make complicated subjects easier for others to grasp.

However, Geminis should remember to be patient. Sometimes, explaining something takes more time than they expect, because not everyone learns at the same pace. If they rush through a lesson, the other person might feel lost. A patient Gemini can be a wonderful helper, guiding someone step by step, while also adding fun facts or stories to keep it interesting.

## Learning a New Language

Geminis might find that learning a new language is exciting for them. They pick up words quickly and often enjoy the process of putting together phrases. If they travel or live in a place where another language is common, they might adapt faster than some others. Their ear for tones and phrases helps them remember vocabulary and grammar rules, especially if they are actively practicing with people who speak that language.

Yet, learning a language still takes dedication and practice. A Gemini might start strongly but risk losing momentum if they do not stay focused. One way to keep the excitement up is to combine language study with fun activities, like watching videos or chatting with native speakers online. By turning it into a social or creative experience, a Gemini might find it easier to stay on track.

## Reading Between the Lines

Geminis can be good at sensing what is not being said in a conversation. They might pick up on little hints that someone is sad or annoyed, even if the person is not showing it openly. This skill comes from their observant nature. They notice small changes in tone of voice or facial expressions. If they sense something off, they might ask, "Are you okay?" or "Is something bothering you?"

However, this skill also depends on how willing the Gemini is to slow down and pay close attention. If they are too busy talking, they might miss these signals. But if they look carefully, they can become quite good at reading people's feelings. This can help them be more caring friends or family members.

## Healthy Boundaries in Conversation

Since Geminis love to share and also ask questions, they might sometimes forget about boundaries. They could poke into personal details without meaning harm, or they might overshare about their own life when the other person is not ready for that much information. Learning when to give people space can be important.

If a Gemini notices that someone seems uncomfortable, they can gently change the topic or say something like, "We don't have to talk about this if it makes you uneasy." Respecting boundaries in conversation can help them keep good relationships. Similarly, Geminis can remember that they do not have to reveal everything about themselves all at once if they are not fully comfortable.

## Encouraging Others to Speak

A Gemini in a group setting can help bring quieter people into the conversation. They might say, "Hey, we haven't heard from you yet—what do you think?" This can make a shy friend feel included. Geminis often enjoy variety, which can also mean hearing a variety of voices. By inviting different people to share, they keep the discussion fresh.

This quality can help Geminis become good leaders in teams or projects. They can ensure that no single person is left out. At the same time, they should be careful not to put someone on the spot if that person truly does not want to speak. Paying attention to social cues can help the Gemini decide who might be ready to talk and who is more comfortable just listening.

## Speaking from the Heart

While Geminis can be logical and playful, they also have feelings that matter. Sometimes, they might avoid serious, heartfelt talks by turning things into jokes or switching topics. But when they truly speak from the heart, they can be very moving. They might share something meaningful or open up about a worry they have.

This can strengthen their bonds with others. It shows that Geminis are not just about quick laughter or random facts—they also have deeper thoughts and feelings. It can be scary to open up, especially for someone who is used to keeping conversations light. But taking that step can build trust and bring a new level of closeness in friendships or family relationships.

## Overcoming Nervousness

Even though many Geminis seem confident, they can still get nervous about talking sometimes, especially if it is a big event or an unfamiliar crowd. They might worry about forgetting what they want to say or not sounding smart enough. However, because they are generally skilled at communication, they can prepare ahead of time to reduce anxiety.

**Some methods include:**

Practicing their speech or presentation in front of a mirror.

Writing out notes to have nearby, just in case they lose their train of thought.

Remembering that even if they slip up, they can adapt quickly.

These steps can help them feel calmer. Once they get into the flow of speaking, most Geminis find that their natural ease with words takes over.

## Remaining Genuine

Because Geminis can adapt to different people, some might worry that a Gemini is not being genuine. They might wonder which "face" is the real one. However, Geminis can learn to remain true to themselves while still adjusting how they speak to others. For example, they can use simpler language with children and a more detailed style with adults, but they can still share their real opinions and feelings in both cases.

Staying genuine also means being honest about what they like and do not like, rather than just going along with the crowd. Geminis can be friendly without losing who they are. Sometimes, it takes self-reflection to figure out how to balance openness to others with staying true to one's own core.

## Handling Criticism

With their many ideas and active style, Geminis might face criticism at times. Perhaps someone thinks they talk too much, or that their jokes are silly. Geminis can be sensitive to harsh words, but they can also use their communication skills to respond in a healthy way. For instance, they can ask for clarity: "Can you explain why you feel that way?" or "What do you think I can improve?"

By staying calm and asking questions, Geminis can turn criticism into a learning moment. Sometimes, they may realize the feedback is fair, and they can adjust. Other times, they may decide that the criticism is not helpful. In either case, handling it calmly shows maturity and keeps the lines of communication open.

## Building Deeper Bonds

Geminis often have a wide circle of acquaintances. They know many people, chat with them, and can seem to be friends with everyone.

However, deep bonds require shared trust and time. If a Gemini wants to build a deeper connection with a few close friends, they can focus on more one-on-one conversations. Listening carefully, sharing personal thoughts, and being consistent in how they treat the other person are key steps.

Spending quality time without distractions can help. For example, a Gemini might put their phone aside for a while and have a face-to-face talk with a friend. They might ask how the friend is really feeling, and then truly hear the answer. By doing this, Geminis can enjoy both their broad social network and a few strong, lasting relationships.

## Conclusion

Communication is often at the core of what makes Geminis shine. They are skilled at talking, writing, and sharing ideas with others. Their quick mind and love of conversation can bring life to any group. They enjoy asking questions, telling jokes, and discussing new ideas. However, it can help them to slow down sometimes, listen fully, and consider the feelings of those around them.

By balancing their natural gifts with awareness and care, Geminis can become amazing communicators. They can learn how to adapt without losing who they are. They can build trust by being honest and open, and they can help others feel heard by asking questions in a thoughtful way. Communication, after all, is not just about speaking—it is also about understanding. And that is something Geminis can do well when they set their minds to it.

With a solid look at how Geminis share ideas, we can now move on to other parts of Gemini life. In the next chapters, we will explore the challenges Geminis face, how they relate to friends and family, and other areas where their talents and traits show up. Each new area will reveal more about what makes Geminis unique, keeping in mind their strong link to words and quick thinking.

# CHAPTER 5: CHALLENGES THAT GEMINI FACES

Geminis have many strong qualities, such as quick thinking and curiosity. Still, like everyone, they can run into problems that keep them from doing their best. In this chapter, we will look at some of the main challenges Geminis might face, why these difficulties happen, and how they might work through them in a simple way. Remember that each person is different. These points may or may not fit every Gemini, but they can help us see common issues that often pop up for people with Gemini traits.

## Restlessness

One of the biggest challenges for many Geminis is restlessness. They may feel bored if they have to do the same task for a long time. For instance, if a Gemini is in a class where the teacher repeats the same material many times, they might start daydreaming. Their mind moves fast and wants new information. This can be tricky in school or in a job that has repetitive tasks.

### Why this Happens

Geminis often have a strong need for variety. Their minds want to jump to new topics before they fully finish the old one. They are curious, and once they have a basic grasp of something, they might want to move on to the next thing.

### Possible Solutions

**Adding small changes**: If a task is long, Geminis might break it into parts. After finishing one part, they can briefly do something different, like getting a drink of water or tidying up their desk. Then they return to the main task.

**Finding new angles**: If they feel stuck on one subject, they can look for a fresh angle to keep it interesting. For example, if they must read a long book for class, they might look up facts about the author or watch a short video about the historical period. This can renew their interest and reduce restlessness.

## Overthinking

Geminis can think very quickly, which is often a strength. But at times, this can spill over into overthinking. They might get stuck in a loop of thoughts, replaying details in their head and asking "What if?" many times. This can show up when they have a decision to make or if they are worried about an event. Their active mind might run in circles, leaving them feeling stressed.

**Why this Happens**

Their strong mental energy can cause them to look at every detail from many angles. While this helps them see lots of possibilities, it also makes it easy to slip into worry. They might imagine every possible outcome and struggle to pick just one path.

**Possible Solutions**

**Writing down thoughts**: A Gemini might ease an overloaded mind by writing out their worries or listing pros and cons for each option. Seeing the ideas on paper can help them see which steps make sense.

**Talking to someone**: Since Geminis are often good at sharing, discussing their concerns with a friend or family member can help them see if they are overthinking. A listener might say, "That idea sounds realistic, but that one is too far-fetched."

## Indecision

Because Geminis can see multiple sides to a problem, they might struggle to pick just one solution. They can get caught between choices, each seeming equally good or equally flawed. For example, a Gemini might spend a lot of time deciding which activity to do on a weekend or which subject to focus on in school. This can be frustrating, both for them and the people around them.

**Why this Happens**

Geminis naturally consider different perspectives. Their curiosity also keeps them open to new options. While it is good to look at all the angles, it can lead to a standoff in their mind if they try to keep every option open for too long.

**Possible Solutions**

**Set a time limit**: Give a certain amount of time to make a choice. For small decisions, that might be just a few minutes. For bigger ones, maybe a few days. Once that time is up, they must pick.

**Trusting their instincts**: Sometimes, Geminis should trust their first reaction. They might remind themselves that no choice is perfect, but they can learn and adjust if needed.

# Lack of Follow-Through

Starting projects is often easy for Geminis because they love new ideas. The hard part can be finishing them. They might begin with a burst of energy, only to lose interest halfway through. This can create a pattern of unfinished plans or half-complete tasks.

**Why this Happens**

Geminis enjoy novelty. Once the newness fades, they might look for fresh excitement. Also, they can get distracted by other interesting topics that appear while they are in the middle of something else.

**Possible Solutions**

**Make the end fun**: If Geminis feel bored in the middle, they can plan a small reward for finishing the project.

**Share goals with someone**: If they tell a friend or family member about what they plan to do, that person might check in. It can be extra motivation to complete the task instead of dropping it.

**Focus on the main purpose**: Reminding themselves why they started the project in the first place can spark excitement again.

## Shallow Knowledge

Because Geminis are curious about many things, they might learn a little bit about a lot of subjects but not go deeper. This is not always bad, but sometimes they might wish to have a deeper skill level in one area. If they skip around too much, they may never master anything.

**Why this Happens**

Geminis are often driven by fresh ideas. Once they feel they know the basics, they are ready to move on. It can be hard for them to stick with one topic long enough to become a true expert.

**Possible Solutions**

**Pick one area to go deeper**: They can choose one subject they truly enjoy and focus on learning more about it. They can still be broad in other areas, but this one subject is where they really spend time.

**Set learning goals**: If they want to deepen their knowledge, they might pick clear goals. For instance, they could say, "I will practice guitar for 15 minutes a day," or "I will read one detailed book on ancient history this month."

## Anxiety About Missing Out

With so many interests, Geminis can worry that they will miss a fun event or interesting subject if they pick something else. They might feel torn when two things happen at once. This fear can cause them to jump from one activity to another, never feeling fully satisfied.

### Why this Happens

Geminis like to be in the know. They are curious about what is going on everywhere, and they do not want to pass up a chance to learn or have fun.

### Possible Solutions

**Accept that you cannot do everything**: Recognize that it is not possible to experience all events or learn all topics. Deciding which ones matter most can bring relief.

**Enjoy the present**: If they choose to attend one event, they can remind themselves to be fully there, rather than thinking about the event they did not attend. Mindful focus can help them get more joy out of each choice.

## Trouble with Routine

Many people like routines, but Geminis can find them stifling if there is no variety. They might skip a daily habit if it feels stale. But some routines are important, like finishing homework on time or keeping their room clean.

### Why this Happens

They enjoy change more than stability. Doing the same exact thing each day might seem dull to a Gemini, so they end up not doing it at all.

### Possible Solutions

**Switch up the routine**: If a Gemini must follow a routine, they can change parts of it. For example, if they must do a task each day, they can do it in a different spot or while listening to different music.

**Make a checklist**: Having a checklist with colorful markers or stickers can make the routine feel slightly more interesting. Each day, they can check off tasks in a playful way.

## Social Exhaustion

Geminis like people and communication, but they can wear themselves out if they try to talk to everyone all the time. They might join many group chats, make plans with lots of friends in one week, or spend hours texting. After a while, they could feel drained.

### Why this Happens
They thrive on variety and interaction, but even the most social person needs a break now and then. Geminis might not notice their own tiredness until it hits them all at once.

### Possible Solutions

**Set boundaries**: Pick times to turn off notifications, or keep the phone in another room for a bit. This gives the mind space to rest.

**Learn to say no**: If a Gemini is invited to multiple social events, it is okay to pick just one or two. Quality time can be better than being spread too thin.

## Handling Deep Emotions

While Geminis can be logical and talkative, they might find it harder to handle deeper feelings, whether their own or someone else's. They could try to lighten the mood with jokes or change the subject, rather than sitting with difficult emotions.

### Why this Happens

Their quick-moving mind might not like the slower, heavier feeling of deep emotion. They may feel uncomfortable or unsure how to respond, so they switch to a safer topic.

### Possible Solutions

**Practice empathy**: When a friend or family member is sad, just listening quietly can help a lot. Geminis do not have to fix the problem with talk; sometimes, kindness and patience are all that is needed.

**Allow themselves to feel**: If a Gemini is sad or worried, they might set aside some time to sit with the feeling. They can write about it, talk to a trusted person, or simply notice it without running away.

## Confusion Over True Desires

Geminis can be pulled in different directions by their wide range of interests. They might ask themselves, "What do I truly want in life? Do I want to be an artist, or do I prefer writing, or maybe something else?" This confusion can last a long time if they keep getting excited by new things without ever deciding what truly fits them best.

### Why this Happens

They see value in many paths. Their flexible mind can envision success in several areas, so they do not want to pick just one.

### Possible Solutions

**Try small tests**: If they are unsure of a big life path, they can do short projects or volunteer to test the waters. This might help them see if they really like that area before diving fully in.

**Reflect on long-term feelings**: They can ask themselves which interests stay strong over time and which fade quickly. If something has kept them interested for many months or years, that might be a clue that it is important.

## Perfectionism in Words

Sometimes, Geminis can get stuck trying to phrase their ideas perfectly. They might spend too long editing a text or rethinking how to say something. While words are their strength, it can also lead to a kind of perfectionism that slows them down.

They value clear communication. They know that words matter. They might also worry about being misunderstood, so they try to craft their statements just right.

**Possible Solutions**

**Accept "good enough"**: Realize that no message will be perfect for every listener. Once they feel it is understandable, they can stop editing.

**Speak naturally**: When possible, speak in person. That way, tone and body language can fill in the gaps that words alone cannot.

## Worry About Being Misunderstood

Geminis often switch styles depending on the situation, and they might worry that people do not see the real person behind these changes. This can lead to a sense of always having to explain or prove themselves.

### Why this Happens

Their adaptable nature can make others question their sincerity. The Gemini may see this and feel stressed, wondering how to show their genuine self.

### Possible Solutions

**Consistency in key values**: Even if they change how they speak or act in different settings, they can keep the same core values. That way, people will see that, no matter the style, the person is the same inside.

**Be patient**: Trust is built over time. If a Gemini keeps showing they are honest, people will begin to see the stable side behind their changing interests.

## Feeling Trapped by Obligations

Geminis can feel trapped if they have many duties that do not allow for creative thinking. For instance, if they have a strict schedule with no room to explore new ideas, they might feel caged. This can lead to frustration or even a desire to drop all obligations.

**Why this Happens**

Their natural state is flexible, so strict structures can clash with their need to adapt and experiment.

**Possible Solutions**

**Plan small creative breaks**: Even if they have big responsibilities, they can give themselves 15-minute windows here and there to do something refreshing, like doodling or reading a fun article.

**Look for ways to improve tasks**: Sometimes, duties can be changed a bit to be more interesting. For example, they could find a new way to organize their work or add a personal twist to a standard project.

## Difficulty Keeping Secrets

Geminis love talking and sharing interesting facts. Sometimes, this can include sharing details that were meant to be private. They might slip up without meaning to, simply because they are used to passing along information.

**Why this Happens**

They naturally see information as something to spread around. They might not realize that certain details are off-limits.

**Possible Solutions**

**Ask for clarity**: If a friend tells them something personal, the Gemini can ask, "Is it okay if I share this with anyone else?" This reminder helps them know what must stay private.

**Pause before speaking**: When about to share something that involves another person, they can pause to consider if it was given in confidence. If they are not sure, they can keep it private.

## Handling Criticism

Geminis can take criticism personally, especially if it is about their communication or ideas. They might respond with a quick defense or try to over-explain. This can make it hard for them to accept feedback calmly.

### Why this Happens

Their ideas and words feel personal to them, so negative comments may sting more. They can also feel that the person criticizing them does not understand the full context.

### Possible Solutions

**Count to three**: When they hear criticism, they can pause for a few seconds before responding. This helps them avoid a knee-jerk reaction.

**Ask questions**: They might say, "Can you tell me more about what you mean?" This can show they are open to learning, and it might reveal that the other person's criticism was not as harsh as it first sounded.

## Moving Too Fast

Geminis' speed is often a gift, but it can also lead them to rush tasks. They might miss important details or instructions because they hurry. This might show up in schoolwork, on tests, or in daily chores.

### Why this Happens

They are used to their minds racing, so they assume their hands and actions should race too. Slowing down can feel unnatural, even though it can lead to better outcomes.

### Possible Solutions

**Check steps**: After finishing a task, they can review it once more. For example, if they complete a math problem, they can read it again to ensure they did not skip any part.

**Use a timer**: When working on something, set a timer for a bit longer than they would normally take. This nudges them to pace themselves more steadily.

## Inconsistent Sleep Schedules

Because Geminis stay busy, their sleep can suffer. They might stay up late chatting online or get distracted by an interesting book. Then, they wake up tired the next day, which affects their focus and mood.

### Why this Happens

They do not want to shut down their mental activity, which often picks up speed at night. There is always one more thing to read or watch.

### Possible Solutions

**Wind-down routine**: An hour before bed, turn off devices and do something calming, like gentle stretching or listening to soft music. This helps signal the mind that it is time to rest.

**Set bedtime reminders**: Having an alarm that says "Time to get ready for bed" can help them remember that rest is necessary, not optional.

## Conflict in Group Work

Geminis often bring creativity to group tasks, but conflicts can arise if others cannot keep up with their changing ideas. The Gemini might present multiple ideas, leading to confusion or tension when the group wants a simpler plan.

### Why this Happens

They want to explore many angles, but not everyone works that way. Some group members might be happier focusing on one idea until it is done.

### Possible Solutions

**Limit idea-sharing**: Before throwing out ten possible approaches, a Gemini might share just two or three. Then ask for feedback. If the group wants more, they can offer more.

**Clarify steps**: Once the group picks a plan, the Gemini can help outline the steps clearly so everyone can agree on the path forward.

## Emotional Pressure from Others

Friends or family might expect the Gemini to always be upbeat and talkative. But Geminis have down days too. They can feel pressure to perform or keep conversations going, which is tiring if they need quiet time.

### Why this Happens

Others see them as lively and expect that to be constant. Geminis might feel guilty if they want to be alone or skip a social event.

### Possible Solutions

**Be honest**: If they need a quiet night, they can politely say, "I'm feeling a bit tired today. Let's hang out another time."

**Remember self-care**: Their energy recharges if they allow themselves breaks from social demands.

## Handling Serious Tasks

Some tasks require a lot of patience and careful planning—like writing a long report or managing a complex project. Geminis might get frustrated if they cannot add excitement or if the topic becomes dull after a while.

### Why this Happens

Their mental style thrives on quick exchanges, so very long, detailed tasks can feel tedious.

**Possible Solutions**

**Work in intervals**: They can do the serious task in chunks, taking a small break between parts. This keeps their energy from dropping too low.

**Ask for help**: If the project has many steps, they might team up with someone more detail-focused, while the Gemini handles the brainstorming side.

## Balancing Alone Time and Social Time

Geminis can either fill their schedule with social events or suddenly withdraw when they get overwhelmed. Balancing these two states can be a challenge. They may not always see the need for alone time until they have no energy left for others.

**Why this Happens**

They enjoy talking, but they might overlook the fact that rest and reflection are also important. They could also feel that being alone is boring if they do not plan what to do with that time.

**Possible Solutions**

**Plan quiet moments**: They can set aside a short period each day to read, draw, or simply relax without pressure.

**Tune in to energy levels**: If they notice feeling worn out, that is a signal to take a break instead of forcing more socializing.

## Fear of Missing New Opportunities

Geminis can worry that if they stick with one path for too long, they will miss a better path elsewhere. This can cause them to hop from one goal to another. They keep searching for the "best" fit, but never settle into a single focus.

**Why this Happens**

They see the world as full of ideas and choices. They fear regret if they pick wrongly, so they avoid settling.

**Possible Solutions**

**Remember that no path is forever**: Choosing something now does not mean they are stuck in it forever. They can switch later if they truly find a better fit.

**Track progress**: If they set a goal and track how far they have come, they might see the rewards of staying with something a bit longer.

## Worries About Being Seen as Inconsistent

Because Geminis can be in one mood one day and another mood the next, they might worry that people see them as flaky. This can be stressful if they want to be known as reliable.

**Why this Happens**

They know they can change quickly, and they sense that others may not understand it. They do not want to lose trust.

**Possible Solutions**

**Communicate changes**: If they change a plan, they can tell others as soon as possible, explaining why. This shows respect for everyone's time.

**Keep promises on key things**: Even if they shift interests often, they can focus on keeping any promises they have made. Over time, people will see that, despite daily changes, the Gemini does not let them down on important matters.

## Self-Doubt

With all the movement in their minds, Geminis can experience waves of self-doubt. They might question whether their ideas are truly good or if people really like being around them. This can happen after a social event or when they compare themselves to people who specialize in one area.

**Why this Happens**

Their flexible nature can lead them to see multiple viewpoints, including negative ones about themselves. They might think, "Someone else is better at this," or "I don't stick to anything, so maybe I'm not good at anything."

**Possible Solutions**

**Focus on strengths**: They can list times when their quick thinking or curiosity helped them achieve something. This reminds them of what they bring to the table.

**Seek feedback**: If they are unsure, they can ask trusted friends or teachers for honest input. Often, they will hear that others do appreciate their fresh ideas and lively nature.

# Conclusion

Geminis face a range of challenges, many of which come from the same traits that make them so bright and engaging. Their curiosity, flexibility, and quick thinking can turn into restlessness, indecision, or anxiety if they are not careful. By noticing these patterns, Geminis can learn how to handle them better. This might involve setting limits, planning breaks, or focusing on a single goal when necessary.

It is important for Geminis to remember that challenges do not make them any less special. They simply point to areas where they can develop healthier habits. A Gemini who is aware of these possible hurdles can make better choices, remain cheerful, and continue sharing their curious spirit with the world. In the next chapter, we will shift our focus to how Geminis behave in friendships—a big part of their social nature and day-to-day life.

# CHAPTER 6: GEMINI IN FRIENDSHIPS

Friendship often plays a major role in a Gemini's life because they enjoy meeting new people and exchanging ideas. This chapter focuses on how Geminis act in friendships, what they look for in a friend, and how they keep—or sometimes lose—these bonds. We will also look at ways Geminis can improve their friendships so that they remain strong and positive for everyone involved.

## First Impressions

When Geminis meet new people, they often leave a strong first impression. They might strike up a lively chat, crack a joke, or ask a thoughtful question. Their quick mind helps them think of interesting topics to discuss, which can make them fun to talk with right away.

### Why They Make Quick Connections

**They enjoy conversations**: Geminis naturally chat, so they can quickly find some common ground.

**They are curious**: They ask questions about the other person's likes and dislikes, which can make the other person feel seen.

This skill often leads to many casual acquaintances, because Geminis are not afraid to start a conversation with strangers. They might do this at school, in clubs, or in online communities.

## Variety of Friends

Because of their wide range of interests, Geminis may collect a variety of friends from different backgrounds. They might have one friend who shares a love of science, another friend who plays music with them, and another friend who just enjoys talking about movies. Geminis are not always picky; if someone can hold a fun or interesting conversation, the Gemini is happy to connect.

**Benefits**

**They learn a lot**: Each friend can teach them something different.

**They can adapt easily**: Switching from one circle to another is not stressful for most Geminis because they are flexible.

**Possible Drawback**

**Hard to spend equal time with everyone**: With so many different friends, Geminis might find it challenging to keep all these connections strong.

## Bringing Energy to the Group

In a group of friends, the Gemini often stirs up excitement. They might suggest fun topics or new activities. They can be the one who keeps the chat lively, jumping in with comments or asking others for their thoughts. People often appreciate this energy, especially in situations where the group might otherwise be quiet.

**Examples**

**Starting new group hobbies**: A Gemini might say, "Let's try a board game none of us have played before," and everyone gets excited.

**Finding unusual topics**: If the group is stuck in small talk, the Gemini might bring up something new they read or a silly fact, leading to fresh laughs or debates.

## The Challenge of Keeping Promises

One problem a Gemini friend might have is following through on the plans they make. They might say, "We should do this cool thing next week!" but then forget or get interested in something else. This can disappoint friends who were looking forward to the plan.

**Why This Happens**

Geminis can get carried away by new ideas. Their initial spark of excitement might fade if something else pulls their attention.

**Ways to Improve**

**Write down the plan**: Mark it on a calendar or phone reminder.

**Check in with the friend**: The Gemini can send a quick message asking if the plan is still on. This helps anchor them to what they said they would do.

## Light-Hearted Teasing

Geminis often engage in light teasing with friends, tossing jokes back and forth. This can be fun and show closeness. However, it can also cause misunderstandings if the friend is sensitive or if the Gemini jokes about a topic that hits a nerve.

**Advice**

**Read the friend's mood**: If the friend seems uneasy, the Gemini can ease off on the teasing.

**Use humor kindly**: Aim to make the friend laugh, not to poke at their insecurities.

When done well, this playful teasing can create a comfortable and fun environment. Geminis just have to be aware of the line between harmless jokes and hurtful remarks.

## Deep vs. Surface Friendships

Geminis can have many friends but may keep the connection on a surface level for a long time. They enjoy chatting and joking, yet they might not share personal problems or deeper feelings easily. Some friends might crave a more meaningful bond, wishing the Gemini would open up.

### Reasons for Surface-Level Bonds

**They like to keep things light**: Too much seriousness can feel heavy for Geminis.

**They worry about losing fun**: They might think that if they get too deep, the friendship will change and not be as easygoing.

### Finding Depth

**Share small pieces of personal life**: They can open up gradually, letting the friend see a bit more of who they are.

**Listen to the friend's deeper thoughts**: If a friend opens up about something important, the Gemini can be supportive. Over time, both might feel safe to have deeper talks.

## Handling Friendship Conflicts

All friendships can have conflicts, and Geminis are no exception. They might argue about shared plans, teasing that went too far, or a misunderstanding in communication. Geminis might try to solve the conflict by talking it out quickly, but sometimes deep feelings need more gentle handling.

### Common Conflict Areas

**Broken plans**: If a Gemini changes their mind too often, friends can feel let down.

**Too many jokes**: If the friend feels teased, they might distance themselves.

### Possible Solutions

**Open communication**: If the Gemini notices tension, they can ask, "Did I do something that upset you?"

**Apologies**: A sincere apology, without trying to gloss over the issue, can heal things fast.

**Taking it seriously**: Some conflicts require more than a quick fix. The Gemini might need to slow down and show genuine concern.

## Being the Connector

Because Geminis mix with many groups, they can act as a bridge. For example, if they know one friend who loves sports and another who also loves sports, they might introduce them. This makes the Gemini a connector who brings people together.

### Why They Enjoy This Role

**They like variety**: They want all sorts of different people to meet each other.

**It feels meaningful**: Helping friends expand their social circles can be fun and fulfilling for a Gemini.

### Challenge

**Balancing group dynamics**: Sometimes, mixing different friend groups can cause friction. A Gemini should check if the two friends want to meet each other and if their personalities might match well.

## Adapting to Different Friends

Geminis often change their communication style depending on who they are with. With a funny friend, they might joke a lot. With a quiet friend, they might talk more calmly about serious topics. This helps them fit into different circles, but it can also raise concerns about authenticity if people notice the changes.

### Why Adaptation Happens

**They are flexible**: They sense what the other person's vibe is and match it.

**They like harmony**: They want to avoid making someone uncomfortable.

### Being Genuine

**Stay true to core values**: Even if they switch styles, their beliefs and kindness can remain the same.

**Explain if needed**: If a friend questions why they act differently around other people, they can say something like, "I just adjust to who I'm with, but I'm still me."

## Friendship Overload

Geminis may end up with so many friends that they spread themselves thin. They might have multiple social events in one week and realize they have no time to rest or tend to personal projects. This can lead to stress or even burnout, where they feel too drained to fully enjoy their friendships.

### Why This Happens

**They love variety**: They do not like turning down invites because everything seems interesting.

**They have a fear of missing out**: They worry a great time might pass them by if they do not accept.

### Handling Overload

**Set priorities**: Choose which invites are most meaningful. It is okay to skip some.

**Plan downtime**: Mark a day or evening on the calendar for quiet rest. If they do not plan it, a Gemini might fill it with more social plans.

## Loyalty Concerns

Because Geminis can shift from friend to friend, some people might doubt their loyalty. They might think, "How can I trust that they will stick around if they keep bouncing between groups?" In reality, many Geminis do care about loyalty. They just show it differently.

### How Geminis Show Loyalty

**They remember small details**: Even if they are not always there, they may recall personal facts about their friends.

**They reach out**: A Gemini might send a quick message just to say hello or check how a friend is feeling.

### Building Trust

**Keep confidences**: If a friend shares something private, a Gemini can show loyalty by not sharing it with others.

**Stay in contact**: Even if they have been busy, a simple message to a friend after some time can keep the bond alive.

## Giving Support

When friends have problems, Geminis might try to help by brainstorming ideas or offering logical advice. They can be good at seeing many possibilities. However, sometimes a friend simply wants empathy rather than quick fixes. Geminis might need to notice when to just listen.

### Steps to Provide Better Support

**Ask how the friend feels**: Before giving solutions, ask about feelings.

**Listen**: Let the friend talk without jumping in too soon.

**Offer help**: If the friend wants ideas, share them. If they just want comfort, keep it simple.

## Handling Quiet Friends

Geminis can be quite talkative, but some of their friends might be more reserved. This can create an interesting balance. The Gemini might feel they are doing all the talking, while the quiet friend might struggle to speak up.

### Tips for Communicating with Quiet Friends

**Ask direct questions**: A gentle "What do you think?" can encourage them to share.

**Give them time**: Quiet friends might need a little longer to respond.

**Value their input**: Show genuine interest in what they say, so they know their words matter.

## Shared Hobbies

Geminis often do well in friendships where there is a shared hobby, like gaming, sports, art, or even just chatting about a topic they both love. This shared interest can keep the bond strong because it gives them an easy way to connect.

### Why Shared Hobbies Help

**They add structure**: Instead of meeting just to talk, friends can meet to play a game or practice a skill.

**They reduce boredom**: Geminis can channel their lively energy into something fun that both friends enjoy.

### Risk of Switching Interests

**Sudden change**: A Gemini might drop a hobby if a new one seems more exciting. The friend could feel abandoned if they were still enjoying the old hobby. Communication is important to keep hurt feelings at bay.

## Generating Group Plans

Geminis often volunteer to make plans for a group of friends. They might come up with a theme night or propose going to a new place. These plans can be creative and exciting. However, the Gemini must also handle the details: who is attending, what time, and how to manage costs.

### How to Succeed

**Delegate tasks**: If the Gemini is not detail-oriented, they can ask a more organized friend to handle some parts.

**Confirm attendance**: A quick group chat or phone call can ensure people actually come.

When done well, the Gemini's knack for ideas can lead to memorable times for everyone.

## Avoiding Friend-Group Drama

With many friends in different circles, Geminis sometimes land in the middle of drama. They might hear gossip from one group, then see another group reacting. It can be stressful to juggle the feelings of multiple sets of people.

**Tips to Avoid Drama**

**Steer clear of gossip**: If a Gemini hears talk about someone else, they can avoid passing it on.

**Be fair**: If two friends are in a disagreement, try not to take sides too quickly. Encourage them to talk it out.

**Set boundaries**: If a group tries to pull the Gemini into negative chatter, they can politely change the subject or say they do not feel comfortable discussing it.

## Patience with Differences

Because Geminis have friends from various backgrounds, they might sometimes face conflicts when two friends have different values or opinions. Geminis can help by encouraging calm talks, but they need patience to handle the tension. They might also worry that the two friends will demand the Gemini pick a side.

**Strategies**

**Promote understanding**: Suggest the friends talk directly instead of complaining to others.

**Stay neutral**: If possible, avoid taking sides unless one friend is clearly in the wrong.

**Accept that not everyone gets along**: Sometimes, two friends just will not click. The Gemini can still keep separate friendships without forcing them together.

## Respecting Introverted Friends

Some of the Gemini's friends might be introverted. They might recharge by having alone time and not enjoy frequent social events. The Gemini should understand this does not mean they dislike the friendship. It only means they need space.

**How to Support Introverted Friends**

**Plan smaller hangouts**: Instead of a big group, invite them for a quiet chat or a one-on-one activity.

**Give notice**: If inviting them to an event, let them know in advance so they can prepare themselves mentally.

**Respect a "no"**: If they decline an invite, do not push. Let them know it is fine.

## Building Long-Term Friendships

While Geminis are quick to form new connections, building lasting friendships requires more effort. Over the years, people grow and change. A Gemini who wants to keep old friends should find ways to stay in contact, even if new interests come along.

### Ideas for Keeping Long-Term Bonds

**Regular check-ins**: Send a simple message: "How are you doing? Miss talking with you."

**Shared memories**: Remind each other of past funny moments or accomplishments that bind you together.

**Adapt together**: If a friend's interests change, the Gemini can look for new overlapping hobbies or simply enjoy hearing about the friend's new passions.

## Balancing Talk and Silence

Geminis can talk a lot when excited. But sometimes, friends want a peaceful moment. Too much chatter can be overwhelming, especially for those who need quiet to think or relax.

### How to Balance

**Pause often**: During a conversation, pause to let the friend speak or to allow a small silence.

**Listen for cues**: If the friend's responses get short or they seem tired, it might be time to slow down.

**Find calm activities**: Suggest an activity that does not require constant talking, like a calm walk in the park or a puzzle.

## Encouraging Friends

Geminis can be good at motivating their friends to try new things because they are enthusiastic about ideas. If a friend is hesitant about learning a new skill or going to an event, a Gemini might say, "You can do it, and I'll come along to support you."

**Positive Impact**

**Boosts confidence**: The friend may feel braver with a Gemini cheering them on.

**Shared fun**: Both get to share an activity they might not have tried otherwise.

**Caution**

**Ensure real support**: If the Gemini promises to stick around, they should do so rather than drifting off to another group once they get there.

## When Friendships End

Not all friendships last forever. A Gemini might drift apart from someone if their interests change a lot. Or maybe a conflict cannot be resolved. Ending a friendship can be sad, even for a Gemini who likes change.

**Ways to Handle an Ending**

**Honesty**: If the Gemini senses the bond has run its course, it can help to politely talk about it. A gentle message like, "It seems we have gone separate ways lately," might bring closure.

**Keeping it polite**: Even if they are no longer close, they do not have to end on bad terms. A calm goodbye can be better than a messy fight.

## Working Together on Projects

Friends often collaborate on school projects, clubs, or other group tasks. A Gemini can bring fresh ideas, but the friend might handle the details. This can be a strong combo.

**Key Points for Success**

**Clear roles**: If the Gemini is the ideas person, let them focus on that. Make sure someone else can be the planner if the Gemini struggles with long-term structure.

**Check in regularly**: The Gemini might lose track of what is done, so friendly check-ins help keep everything on course.

## Being Mindful of Friend's Emotions

Geminis are good at sharing facts and ideas, but they must remember that friends have feelings that need attention. If a friend is upset, the Gemini should not jump right to logical solutions or jokes.

### Helpful Steps

**Ask how they feel**: A simple "How are you holding up?" can open the door.

**Listen more than talk**: Let the friend express themselves.

**Offer comfort**: A kind word or a caring gesture can mean a lot.

## Conclusion

Friendships are a key part of many Geminis' lives. They love meeting new people, sharing ideas, and bringing fun to group settings. They can adapt to different social circles and inspire friends to try fresh activities. Yet, challenges arise when they overbook themselves, forget plans, or stay only on the surface of friendships without deeper bonds.

By balancing their social energy, keeping promises, and listening well, Geminis can form strong and loyal friendships. They can learn to handle conflicts with patience and avoid the trap of always looking for something more exciting elsewhere. If they remember to be genuine and open up sometimes, they can enjoy both a wide circle of acquaintances and a few close friends they can rely on.

In the next chapters, we will look at how Geminis interact with family, do in school, and handle other aspects of daily life. Friendships are just one part of that, but an important one, since Geminis thrive when they feel connected to others.

# CHAPTER 7: GEMINI IN THE FAMILY

Geminis often show their curious and talkative traits in family life. They might chat constantly, crack jokes, ask many questions, or share interesting facts. In this chapter, we will look at how Geminis behave around parents, siblings, and other relatives. We will talk about the ways Geminis can add fun to the family setting, as well as possible conflicts that might arise. We will also give simple ideas that may help Geminis and their family members get along better. The goal is to provide new information about Geminis in the family without repeating what we have already covered in earlier chapters.

## Needing Mental Stimulation at Home

One key Gemini trait is the need for new ideas. At home, this can show up in how they like to do different things each day. A Gemini child or teen might move from playing a computer game to reading an article, then switch to chatting with a parent. This can be both exciting and overwhelming for family members who prefer a calmer atmosphere.

**Possible Household Effect**: If a Gemini is always coming up with random facts or sharing new ideas during dinnertime, it can keep the family conversation lively. Parents might be glad to see such interest in the world. However, some family members might feel tired if the Gemini never stops talking or changes the topic too fast.

**Helpful Tip**: Families can set aside a short period each day—maybe at the dinner table or during a shared break—where the Gemini can talk about something new they learned or found interesting. This gives them a special time to share. Afterward, they can practice listening to others and hearing about their day.

## Bonding with Parents

Geminis tend to bond best with parents who welcome questions and enjoy communication. If a parent is open to discussing various topics, from silly to serious, the Gemini will likely feel understood. On the other hand, if a parent gets annoyed by too many questions, the Gemini might feel frustrated or bored.

**How Parents Can Connect**:

**Engage in Small Talks**: Ask the Gemini what they discovered that day or what made them curious.

**Encourage Interests**: If a Gemini shows sudden interest in a new hobby, a parent can show support by asking about it, or providing simple resources if possible.

**Set Boundaries Gently**: If a Gemini is talking too much at a time when parents are busy, the parent can say, "I want to hear about this. Let's chat in 10 minutes when I'm free." This way, the Gemini does not feel shut out.

**Challenge**: If a parent is very quiet or does not like to discuss things in depth, a Gemini might feel a gap. This can lead the Gemini to share more with siblings, friends, or other relatives instead. It might help if the parent simply tries to join in occasional discussions, even if it is just for a little while.

## Typical Gemini Roles in the Family

Within a household, a Gemini might show certain patterns, whether they are the oldest, youngest, or somewhere in the middle. Here are some possible roles they might play:

**The Family Messenger**: Because Geminis often like to talk, they can be the go-between among different members of the family. They might run to a sibling's room with a message or tell one parent what the other parent said. Sometimes this is helpful; other times, it might stir up confusion if they add their own spin to the message.

**The Idea Starter**: Geminis might suggest trying out new things at home, like changing the furniture arrangement or starting a small cooking experiment. They can bring fresh energy to family routines.

**The Talkative Entertainer**: When relatives visit, the Gemini might take the lead in telling jokes or interesting stories. They enjoy making gatherings more lively.

## Relationship with Siblings

If a Gemini has siblings, the nature of the relationship can vary based on many factors, like age differences and personalities. In general, Geminis tend to be playful and curious with siblings, but they can also clash if they feel the sibling is too serious or not open to new ideas.

**Positive Aspects**:

**Shared Activities**: A Gemini might come up with fun games for siblings to play, keeping them from being bored.

**Communication**: Geminis can sometimes help siblings talk through problems. They might ask questions and offer suggestions.

**Possible Struggles**:

**Teasing**: A Gemini might tease a sibling without knowing they have gone too far.

**Shifting Attention**: A Gemini might promise to do an activity with a sibling but get distracted by something else, leaving the sibling disappointed.

To keep sibling ties strong, Geminis can learn to respect their siblings' feelings and schedules. They might need to set reminders for shared plans so they do not forget. Siblings can also remember that the Gemini's quick shifts in attention are not meant to ignore them—Geminis just have many interests.

## Helping with Family Tasks

In many families, everyone shares chores or duties, like cleaning dishes, walking the dog, or taking out the trash. Geminis might do these tasks willingly at first if they see it as something fresh or slightly different each time. But if the chore feels too repetitive, they could lose interest quickly.

**Encouraging a Gemini to Help**:

**Add Variety**: For example, if a Gemini is supposed to clean their room, the parent might let them rearrange the furniture once in a while. This makes the job feel less like the same old routine.

**Set Clear Times**: If a chore has a deadline, the Gemini can plan around it instead of leaving it unfinished.

**Offer Small Breaks**: Breaking chores into short bursts can help a Gemini stay interested.

**Possible Pitfall**: The Gemini might see a new topic online or get a text from a friend and forget their chore halfway through. A simple reminder from a parent or sibling can bring them back on task.

## Handling Family Rules

Geminis often like freedom to follow their curiosity, so strict family rules might feel restrictive. For example, if there is a rule like "No phone at the dinner table," a Gemini who is used to checking messages might feel uneasy. Yet, they can also see the logic if it is explained clearly.

**Listening to Rules**: Geminis are more likely to listen if they understand the reason. If the parent explains, "We do not use phones at dinner so we can talk face to face," the Gemini may respect it because it is about real conversation—a topic Geminis often enjoy.

**Adapting**: If a Gemini finds a rule too strict, they can politely discuss it with the parent. Because Geminis talk well, they might explain why they feel the rule could be adjusted. Sometimes, they can reach a compromise if they stay calm and respectful.

## Dealing with Family Conflicts

Family conflicts happen in all homes. For Geminis, these conflicts might center on issues like forgetting chores, teasing a sibling, or talking back. When conflict arises, Geminis often try to solve it through words, but emotions in family fights can run high.

**Advice for Geminis**:

**Slow Down**: It might help to pause and not speak right away if tempers are hot. Geminis can gather their thoughts before responding.

**Acknowledge Feelings**: Instead of trying to fix things right away, they can say, "I see you're upset. Let's talk about it."

**Be Flexible**: If a sibling or parent has a different view, Geminis can use their ability to see multiple sides to find common ground.

**Advice for Family Members**:

**Be Clear and Calm**: Because Geminis can react fast, it helps if parents or siblings are direct about what is bothering them.

**Avoid Long Speeches**: If a parent lectures for a long time, the Gemini might zone out. Short, clear points are more effective.

## Sharing Personal Space

In a household, rooms or certain areas might be shared, especially if siblings have to share a bedroom. A Gemini might fill the space with books, gadgets, or hobby items and switch them around often. This can annoy a sibling who likes a more tidy area.

**Organizing Together**: A schedule for cleaning can help. For instance, every weekend, siblings can straighten up their shared space. Geminis might find it easier if they can arrange items in different ways, so the chore does not become stale.

**Respecting Privacy**: Geminis might be curious and look through a sibling's stuff or ask many questions about it. They should learn to respect the sibling's boundaries. If the sibling does not want certain items touched, the Gemini should follow that.

## Meal Times and Conversations

Geminis typically love to discuss events of the day, fun topics, or random facts during meals. This can bring life to family dining. Sometimes, though, they might dominate the talk, leaving others without a chance to speak.

**Tips for Balance**:

**Ask Round-Robin Questions**: The family can go around the table, letting each member share something. That way, the Gemini has space to chat, and others do too.

**Keep Topics Varied**: Geminis can easily do this by switching subjects. Just be sure to let others finish their thoughts.

When everyone has a turn to talk, mealtime can be a pleasant time for the family to connect.

## Extended Family Gatherings

When cousins, grandparents, or other relatives visit, Geminis might shine as the ones who spark conversation. They can keep everyone entertained with jokes or tidbits of information. They may also float from group to group, chatting with many relatives because they enjoy variety.

**Building Bonds**:

**Stories**: Geminis might ask grandparents to share memories from the past, turning it into a lively back-and-forth exchange.

**Activities**: Suggesting a simple group game can bring laughter. The Gemini might explain the rules quickly, as they like to share information.

**Caution**: Too many jokes or teasing can lead to misunderstandings, especially if older relatives do not share the same sense of humor. Geminis should pay attention to cues and be ready to switch topics if the mood seems off.

## Respect for Different Generations

Geminis often adapt their conversation style to fit the person they are speaking with. Around elders, they might try to be polite and thoughtful, while around younger siblings, they can be more playful. This skill can help them communicate with relatives of all ages, but it also requires sensitivity.

**Talking to Elders**: A Gemini might ask about their experiences and show curiosity about how life was in earlier times. This can make older relatives feel valued.

**Talking to Younger Family Members**: A Gemini can simplify complex thoughts or instructions so children can follow. This might include telling fun stories or engaging them in easy games.

## Emotional Support Within the Family

Geminis tend to focus on ideas, but they are capable of giving emotional support when they notice a family member is sad or stressed. They might approach it by asking questions: "What happened?" or "How are you feeling?" Then they might try to offer a few solutions, since they like to solve problems with words.

**Things to Watch Out For**:

**Listening More**: Sometimes, a family member just needs to share feelings without hearing solutions right away. The Gemini can practice staying quiet and nodding.

**Gentle Words**: Because Geminis can be direct, they should choose words carefully if someone is very upset.

When used well, a Gemini's communication skill can be a big comfort to relatives who need someone to talk to.

## Encouraging a Gemini's Interests at Home

If a Gemini feels stifled at home, they may become restless or moody. Encouraging them to follow a hobby or read about different subjects can help them stay content. Parents do not have to buy expensive tools or gadgets; even simple items can spark the Gemini's imagination.

**Ideas for Support**:

**Reading Space**: Having a cozy spot for reading or doing research might keep a Gemini happy.

**Allow Creative Expression**: If the Gemini wants to write, draw, or do a small project, a parent can offer basic supplies or a quiet corner.

**Ask Follow-Up Questions**: When the Gemini shares something they learned, show real interest. This simple act can mean a lot.

## Handling Household Routines

Daily routines, such as set bedtime or homework time, can feel restrictive to Geminis if there is no room for spontaneity. Yet, routines are often important for a stable family life. Balancing a sense of order with the Gemini's need for change can be tricky.

**Possible Compromises**:

**Flexible Schedule**: Instead of doing homework at exactly 5 PM each day, maybe the Gemini can choose any one-hour slot before dinner to complete it.

**Variation in Tasks**: If there are multiple chores, let the Gemini pick which chore to do first each day. They still have to do them all, but in an order they choose.

## Teaching Responsibility

Geminis sometimes struggle with finishing tasks or sticking to one plan. At home, parents can help them practice responsibility in small steps. For example, giving them a daily job—like feeding a pet—can teach them to follow through. If the Gemini forgets, a gentle reminder can help them remember why it matters.

**Short-Term Goals**: Parents might set simple weekly goals for the Gemini, such as cleaning their own room without being asked. Then, at the end of the week, the family can talk about how it went.

**Positive Reinforcement**: When the Gemini does follow through, a few kind words like, "Nice job finishing that before the deadline," can encourage them to keep it up.

## Gemini's Need for Personal Space

Even though Geminis like talking and social contact, they also need personal space to think or explore ideas on their own. A family that constantly demands the Gemini's attention might see pushback. The Gemini might shut themselves in their room or become unresponsive if they feel overwhelmed.

**Respecting Solitude**: If a parent sees the Gemini reading or writing quietly, it might be good to let them be for a bit. Geminis can recharge mentally in these moments.

**Balancing Time Together**: Family meals and shared activities are still important, but they do not have to fill every hour. Let the Gemini have some freedom.

## Interacting with Different Family Personalities

In any family, personalities can clash. If a sibling or parent is very organized and structured, they might find the Gemini's quick changes annoying. Alternatively, if another family member is very serious, they might see the Gemini's jokes as silly or distracting.

**Finding Middle Ground**: The Gemini can agree to keep certain areas (like the living room) more organized, while they can have more freedom in their own bedroom. If a parent is serious, the Gemini can learn to lighten up but also respect the times when seriousness is needed.

**Listening to Feedback**: If a family member says, "That constant switching of plans is stressing me," the Gemini can try to slow down or give notice before they change something.

## Gemini as Older Sibling

If a Gemini is the older sibling, they might step into a mentor role in certain situations. They could show the younger ones how to do homework, or explain how to perform a particular household task. Because Geminis like to share knowledge, they might enjoy this.

**Advice**:

**Be Patient**: Younger siblings learn at different speeds. A Gemini should not get frustrated if the lesson takes longer than they expect.

**Avoid Too Much Teasing**: Joking can be fun, but repeated teasing might hurt a younger sibling's feelings.

Being an older sibling can be a good match for a Gemini if they remember to be gentle and encouraging rather than impatient.

## Gemini as Younger Sibling

If a Gemini is the younger sibling, they might look up to older siblings for guidance. At the same time, they might question everything an older sibling says because they tend to be curious. This can lead to lively debates at home.

**Advice**:

**Listen Sometimes**: The older sibling might really know more about certain topics. The Gemini can benefit from hearing them out.

**Shared Activities**: The younger Gemini might invite their older sibling to do something fresh or interesting, adding new spark to their bond.

When done right, a Gemini younger sibling can bring energy into the relationship, and the older sibling can provide steady knowledge.

## Navigating Teen Years

During the teen years, a Gemini might face many changes in hobbies, friend groups, and personal style. This can be confusing for parents who cannot keep track of what the Gemini likes one week to the next. However, it can also be a fun time of discovery if the family goes with the flow but still keeps safe limits.

**How Parents Can Help**:

**Offer Guidance Without Limiting Growth**: If the Gemini wants to try a new sport or club, let them, but also remind them not to drop important commitments.

**Check In About Feelings**: Teens can go through emotional ups and downs. A Gemini might hide deeper feelings behind humor. Asking simple questions can help them open up.

**Stay Informed**: Parents can keep a gentle watch on the Gemini's friend groups and interests, making sure nothing harmful is going on, but without being overly strict.

## Emotional Ups and Downs at Home

Geminis can have mood swings due to their quick-thinking nature. They might be cheerful in the morning, then suddenly quiet or grumpy by the afternoon, especially if something did not go well. Family members might be confused by these mood changes.

**Helping with Mood Shifts**:

**Encourage Breaks**: A short walk outside or a moment to listen to music can help a Gemini adjust when they feel stressed.

**Honest Communication**: If a Gemini is upset, saying a simple phrase like, "I'm in a bad mood right now," can help the family understand. Then they can be patient rather than taking it personally.

## Celebrations and Gatherings

During festive family times or special dinners, Geminis can be the ones to spark fun. They might suggest games, share stories, or keep the atmosphere bright. This can bring everyone closer, as long as the Gemini also allows others to speak.

**Engaging Activities**:

**Trivia Games**: Geminis often like trivia since they gather random facts. They can create simple quizzes for the family.

**Funny Stories**: They might share amusing things they saw or heard recently, entertaining older and younger relatives alike.

These events can be a good opportunity for Geminis to connect with everyone and show their friendly side.

## Digital Life with Family

Many Geminis like to communicate online, whether through texting or social media. Parents might set rules about screen time or phone use. The Gemini might agree, as long as they see a reason for those rules.

**Possible Rules**:

**No Phones at Meals**: This gives the family a chance to talk without distractions.

**Device-Free Hour**: A set time each day (or week) for reading, board games, or family chats.

**Internet Safety**: Parents might remind the Gemini about online safety, since Geminis are curious and might explore many websites.

Geminis can benefit from this balance, as it keeps them from getting lost in endless digital chatter and helps them connect more with family members in person.

## Gemini's Future Plans and Family Support

As Geminis grow older, they might jump between different ideas about their future. One month they are interested in one career path, then switch to something totally different. This can worry parents who want a stable direction for their child.

**Family Response**:

**Stay Open-Minded**: Understand that Geminis often need to sample different possibilities before settling on one.

**Encourage Incremental Steps**: If a Gemini shows interest in a field, the family can suggest they do short-term tasks related to that field. This helps them see if they truly like it.

**Set Gentle Goals**: Rather than forcing them to pick one path right away, parents can help them set small goals to gather more information about each interest.

This approach allows Geminis to feel supported as they decide what suits them best.

# CHAPTER 8: GEMINI IN SCHOOL

School is a place where Geminis can show both their best qualities and some of their challenges. They may excel in certain subjects, form many friendships, and bring fresh ideas to the classroom. At the same time, they can also struggle with focusing on long tasks, handling boredom, or following rigid rules. In this chapter, we will look at how Geminis fit into the school environment, how they learn, and how they can overcome academic and social bumps along the way.

## Curiosity as a Strength

Geminis are known for their love of knowledge, which can be a huge advantage in school. They often ask questions, read widely, and pick up new facts quickly.

**In the Classroom**: When a teacher introduces a new subject—like a chapter in science—Geminis might raise their hands first, eager to learn more or share something they already know.

**Homework Approach**: If the homework is about a topic that sparks their interest, Geminis can be very thorough. They might look up extra details, watch short videos, or find new sources to satisfy their curiosity.

The main point is that Geminis rarely run out of questions. If a teacher welcomes questions, the Gemini can develop strong academic skills.

## Challenges with Repetitive Work

While Geminis can do very well with fresh material, they might become restless if the class repeats the same skill or topic for too long. They may complain that they already understand it or that it is dull.

**Effect on School**: A Gemini might stop paying attention if the teacher goes over something too many times. They might doodle in their notebook or chat with classmates. This can lead to missing key details, even though they think they already know the material.

**Possible Solution**: If the teacher allows it, Geminis can ask if they can work on an extension activity once they grasp the main lesson. This keeps them engaged without making them redo things they already understand.

## Group Projects

Many classrooms require group work. Geminis often shine here because they can bring in good ideas and keep the team talking. They might gather information from different sources and propose creative ways to present the project.

**Strengths**:

**Discussion Leader**: They spark brainstorming sessions and make sure everyone's ideas are heard.

**Adaptability**: If a group member has a different idea, the Gemini can find a way to combine it with their own.

**Weaknesses**:

**Following Through**: If the project takes a long time, the Gemini might start strong but lose steam later.

**Taking Over**: Because they talk so much, they might overshadow quieter classmates.

Balancing speaking and listening is key. Letting each team member have clear tasks can help a Gemini stay on track until the project is finished.

## Handling Boredom in Class

When Geminis get bored, they might fidget, daydream, or whisper to friends. Some might pass notes or draw cartoons in the margins of their notebook. This can disrupt the class if the teacher notices or if it distracts classmates.

**Strategies to Cope:**

**Active Note-Taking:** Geminis can keep their minds busy by writing down interesting points or even sketching quick diagrams related to the lesson.

**Ask Thoughtful Questions:** If the teacher is open to it, the Gemini can pose questions that dig a bit deeper into the topic. This helps them stay engaged.

**Focus Challenges:** They can set small goals like, "I will listen closely for the next five minutes," then have a short mental break, then focus again.

## Excelling in Language-Based Subjects

Geminis often do well in classes that involve words: language arts, literature, creative writing, or even debates. They like to express ideas and may find it natural to string words together.

**Why This Happens:** Geminis often have a feel for language. They can sense tone, style, and creative twists in writing.

**Activities They Might Enjoy:**

**Reading Clubs:** Sharing views on books or short stories.

**Public Speaking:** Presenting topics or giving small speeches.

**Writing Assignments:** Whether it is poetry, essays, or short stories, Geminis can have a flair for putting words down in a lively way.

However, if the teacher demands very strict formats or repetitive grammar exercises, a Gemini might lose enthusiasm. It can help if they see each assignment as a chance to learn something new rather than just a chore.

## Interest in Many Clubs

Geminis might sign up for multiple clubs or after-school activities because they love variety. They could join drama club, chess club, and science club all at once, excited by each one's possibilities.

**Benefits**:

**Social Expansion**: They meet different groups of students and form many connections.

**Broadened Knowledge**: Each club feeds a different side of their curiosity.

**Possible Problem**: Overcommitment. If they join too many activities, they might end up rushing from one meeting to another, doing none of them justice. A Gemini can learn to pick two or three clubs they truly care about, giving those activities the proper time and attention.

## Handling Deadlines

Geminis can struggle with deadlines if they become distracted by other interests. For example, they might have a paper due in a week, but they get fascinated by a different topic and forget the due date until it is almost too late.

**Tips for Meeting Deadlines**:

**Use a Planner**: Writing down when each assignment is due can keep them on schedule.

**Break Tasks into Steps**: If it is a big project, set smaller goals with their own mini-deadlines.

**Ask for Help**: Sometimes, a friend or parent can remind them when something is due. While Geminis might want to do it alone, a nudge can prevent late work.

## Talking in Class

Geminis may love to chat with friends during lessons. While this can be harmless in group work, it can be disruptive when the teacher needs quiet. Teachers often have to remind Geminis to hold their thoughts until the right time.

**Ways to Control Excessive Talking**:

**Silent Periods**: The teacher might set short times for quiet study, and the Gemini can treat it as a personal challenge to stay silent.

**Note It Down**: If a thought comes to the Gemini's mind, they can jot it on paper to share later instead of blurting it out right away.

**Seat Placement**: Sometimes, it helps if they do not sit next to their best friend. They can still talk at breaks.

## Social Circle at School

Geminis typically have broad social circles. They might chat with classmates from different grades or friend groups. This can give them many connections, but it can also spread them thin. They might not have enough time to keep every friendship strong.

**Balancing Friendships**:

**Quality vs. Quantity**: A Gemini might reflect on which friendships mean the most and spend extra time with those people.

**Managing Cliques**: If there are cliques at school, a Gemini might move between them, but they should be mindful not to carry gossip from one group to another.

## Being the Class Entertainer

Some Geminis like to crack jokes or make witty comments when the teacher says something. This can make classmates laugh and see the Gemini as fun. However, it can also annoy teachers if it happens too often, especially during serious lessons.

**Advice**:

**Read the Room**: Notice if the teacher or classmates seem annoyed.

**Use Humor Wisely**: A well-timed joke or clever remark can lighten the mood, but too many can disrupt learning.

**Respect Class Rules**: If the teacher has a strict approach, the Gemini can save jokes for break times or group activities where humor is more welcome.

## Focus on Practical Projects

Geminis often enjoy hands-on activities, as long as they involve learning something new. In science class, for example, they might love doing experiments that let them see results right away. In art, they may enjoy creating a piece that shows their unique perspective.

**Why Hands-On Helps**:

**Immediate Results**: Geminis appreciate quick feedback. Doing a project that produces a visible result can keep them engaged.

**Room for Creativity**: They can add personal touches to the project, avoiding strict repetition.

When a teacher combines theory with practice, Geminis can thrive. They might be more willing to read background material if they know they will soon apply it in a project or experiment.

## Navigating School Rules

Some schools have strict rules, like uniforms, timed breaks, or set procedures. Geminis might feel restricted by these. They could grumble about the lack of freedom. Yet, they can still find ways to fit in without constantly breaking rules.

**Strategies**:

**Suggest Improvements**: If Geminis believe a rule can be adjusted, they can politely propose changes to a teacher or student council, using calm, logical points.

**Personalize Within Limits**: If uniforms are mandatory, maybe they can wear a unique but acceptable accessory. This small change can satisfy their urge for variety.

By blending their adaptability with respect for the school's rules, Geminis can avoid unnecessary conflicts.

## Handling Criticism from Teachers

When teachers critique their work, Geminis might feel pressured or misunderstood. They might defend their ideas or speak quickly in an attempt to clarify. However, school is a place where feedback is common, and learning to accept it calmly can help them improve.

**Tips for Taking Feedback**:

**Listen Completely**: Wait for the teacher to finish their explanation.

**Ask Questions**: "Could you show me an example?" or "What exactly should I change?"

**Try It Out**: Before deciding the feedback is wrong, attempt the teacher's suggestion. If the result is better, the Gemini gains new skills.

## Mastering Time Management

Geminis might overestimate how quickly they can finish assignments, especially if they have many interests competing for their time. They might end up working late at night, which affects their rest and their mood at school the next day.

**Methods to Improve**:

**Create a Simple Schedule**: List each subject and the time needed for homework.

**Check Off Tasks**: Seeing tasks completed can motivate Geminis to keep going.

**Reward System**: They might set small rewards after finishing a task on time, like a short break or listening to a favorite song.

## Testing and Exams

When it comes to tests, Geminis may do well if the questions require creative thinking or quick recall of facts. However, they can struggle with slow, detailed problems that need careful step-by-step work, especially in math or subjects with lots of data to process.

**Study Strategies**:

**Use Variety**: Instead of studying from the same notes for hours, switch methods—like reading a summary, then watching an educational clip, then discussing with a friend.

**Practice Slowing Down**: On tests that need detailed solutions, they can practice going through each step carefully, checking for mistakes.

**Anticipate Boredom**: If the subject feels dull, they might spice it up by turning the study session into a game or quiz themselves with flashcards.

## School Social Events

Geminis usually enjoy school social events like dances, fun fairs, or informal gatherings. They can be found chatting with many people, making jokes, or starting small group games. Their lively nature can help others loosen up.

**Advice for Avoiding Overwhelm**:

**Don't Overbook**: If there are multiple events in one week, it might be wise to pick the ones that matter most.

**Be Mindful of Cliques**: A Gemini might float between different friend circles. This is fine, but they should be careful not to accidentally cause tension by repeating private talks from one group to another.

## Being a Peer Helper

Because Geminis like to explain things, they might volunteer as a peer helper or tutor if the school offers such programs. They can show classmates how to understand a topic, or break down a concept into smaller bits.

**Keys to Success**:

**Remember Patience**: The classmate might take longer to grasp the topic than the Gemini expects.

**Avoid Going Too Fast**: A Gemini might jump ahead if they see the answer quickly. Slowing down ensures the other person can follow.

## Seeking Out New Knowledge

Outside of class, Geminis might roam the library, browse interesting online sources, or talk to teachers about extra topics not in the curriculum. This curiosity can lead them to discover fields they really enjoy.

**Examples**:

**Science Experiments**: They might try small projects at home that they read about, then bring the results to school to show classmates.

**Writing for the School Paper**: A Gemini might enjoy covering events or writing opinion pieces, since it uses their words and quick research skills.

Such activities keep them mentally active and can connect them with teachers who appreciate eager learners.

## Handling Class Presentations

Class presentations are often where Geminis excel. They can speak confidently, add humor, and keep the class interested. Some classmates might even look forward to the Gemini's turn to present because it is likely to be entertaining.

**Suggestions for Great Presentations**:

**Stay Organized**: Although they are talkative, they should plan main points so they do not lose track.

**Use Visuals**: Pictures, charts, or short video clips can maintain interest and structure.

**Manage Time**: It is easy for a Gemini to talk too long. Having an outline and a timer helps them finish on schedule.

## Friendships with Teachers

Geminis can form friendly ties with teachers who appreciate curiosity. They might visit a teacher after class to ask more questions or share something cool they found in a book. This can help them get extra guidance.

**Boundaries**: Teachers are authority figures, so the Gemini must stay respectful. While they can talk openly, they should remember the teacher has other duties and cannot always chat at length.

**Long-Term Gain**: A good teacher-student bond might lead to advice about future studies or recommendations for certain clubs or events that match the Gemini's strengths.

## Organization of School Materials

Geminis sometimes have messy backpacks or lockers because they place different papers in random spots. This can lead to lost assignments or confusion about which notebook contains what. With so many interests, they may not prioritize tidiness.

**Easy Ways to Organize**:

**Color Coding**: Use different colored folders or labels for each subject.

**Weekly Cleanup**: Spend a few minutes on the last day of the week tidying up the locker or backpack.

**Digital Helpers**: If the school allows digital tools, Geminis can store notes and tasks in apps where they can be more structured.

## Respecting Classmates' Feelings

Geminis can be quick-witted, and sometimes their jokes or teasing might hurt a classmate's feelings. They might not mean harm, but they should learn to watch for signs that someone feels picked on.

**Being Aware**: If a classmate looks uncomfortable or upset, the Gemini can apologize or change the subject. They can also ask privately if they went too far.

**Knowing Limits**: Good-natured teasing might be fine among close friends, but it can be seen as rude if someone does not welcome it.

## Taking on School Leadership Roles

Some Geminis might run for student council or become group leaders in class projects. Their communication style can help them present ideas and gain classmates' support. However, these roles also require consistency and follow-through.

**Leading Effectively**:

**Delegate Tasks**: Do not try to do it all alone. Share tasks with other members.

**Regular Check-Ins**: Keep track of progress on each goal so nothing is forgotten.

**Stay Open to Feedback**: Classmates might have concerns. Geminis should listen carefully and adapt when needed.

# Dealing with School Stress

Geminis may take on too many activities or overthink certain classes, leading to stress. They might also find themselves unable to decide which projects to focus on first, causing last-minute panic.

**Methods to Reduce Stress**:

**Setting Priorities**: List out tasks in order of importance, handling the highest priority first.

**Short Breaks**: After completing a chunk of homework, they can take a short rest to recharge.

**Talking to a Counselor**: If stress becomes too heavy, a school counselor might offer tips on time management or dealing with anxiety.

# Conclusion

Geminis can experience both highs and lows in the school environment. Their lively minds and love of conversation often make them stand out in class discussions, group projects, and presentations. They can spark fun and fresh perspectives, helping classmates and teachers look at topics in new ways. On the other hand, Geminis might face issues with boredom, short attention spans, overcommitment to clubs, or messy organization. Finding a healthy balance is key.

By using simple strategies like breaking tasks into smaller steps, staying mindful of deadlines, and knowing when to listen rather than talk, Geminis can shine without becoming overwhelmed. Their talent for words and wide-ranging interests can help them excel in language-based subjects, creative tasks, and group collaborations. With practice, they can also learn to handle more detailed or repetitive work by injecting it with small doses of variety. School then becomes a space where Geminis can gather knowledge, form meaningful friendships, and develop the skills they need for future success.

# CHAPTER 9: GEMINI EMOTIONS

Geminis are often seen as bright, talkative, and quick-thinking. At first glance, some people might assume that Geminis only stay on the surface of emotions, flipping from mood to mood without going deeper. But just like everyone else, Geminis do have a full range of feelings, which can include joy, sadness, excitement, worry, frustration, and more. The way Geminis handle these emotions might look different from how other signs do it, mostly because of their active minds and tendency to see many sides of a situation.

In this chapter, we will explore how Geminis experience emotions, why they can shift quickly from one mood to another, and what might help them deal with strong feelings. We will also look at how Geminis show care to others and how they handle challenges like anxiety or feeling low. By reading about Gemini emotions, you can better understand the inner world of this sign—even if, on the outside, Geminis often seem focused on facts or conversations rather than feelings.

## The Dual Nature of Gemini Emotions

Geminis are famously linked with the idea of "twins." In emotional terms, this can mean they experience more than one feeling at once or switch from one feeling to another fairly quickly. For example, a Gemini might wake up excited about a plan for the day but then, an hour later, feel nervous about something unexpected that happened. A short time after that, they could be laughing with friends, only to become thoughtful and quiet moments later. To an observer, this might look inconsistent. However, for Geminis, it often feels natural to move through these moods.

### Why the Change Can Be Sudden

**Active Minds**: Geminis have busy thought processes. A single idea or memory can spark a new emotion, leading them to shift their mood.

**High Sensitivity to Information**: They notice details in their surroundings—like a friend's frown or a teacher's tone of voice—which can quickly affect how they feel.

**Love of Variety**: Since Geminis like new experiences, they can sometimes seek out emotional changes, even if it is not conscious. A small twist in the day's events can cause them to pivot emotionally, simply because it brings fresh feelings.

## Expressing Feelings Through Words

Many Geminis rely on talking to work through what they feel. If something is bothering them, they might chat with friends or family to get it off their chest. If they are happy, they might jump onto social media or text a bunch of people about what made them laugh or smile. Verbal expression can serve as a way for Geminis to process emotions.

**Pros of This Approach**

**Clarity**: Speaking aloud can help Geminis sort through confusion, as they can name their feelings and see them more clearly.

**Connection**: When they share with others, they often get support or advice, which helps them handle emotions better.

**Relief**: Talking can reduce tension and keep feelings from building up too much.

**Possible Drawbacks**

**Oversharing**: A Gemini might tell too many details to too many people if they are not careful.

**Talking Too Soon**: Sometimes, they might speak in the heat of the moment and say things they regret later if they do not pause to reflect first.

## Balancing Logic and Emotion

Geminis often view the world through a mental lens. They might try to analyze emotions logically, breaking them down into reasons or looking for quick fixes. This can be useful in certain situations, especially if the emotions relate to a practical problem. For instance, if a Gemini feels anxious about a school project, they might handle the feeling by listing the steps needed to finish it.

### Benefits

**Problem-Solving**: Geminis can focus on what they can do to reduce stress.

**Avoiding Emotional Overwhelm**: Turning feelings into something they can fix can keep them from feeling powerless.

### Challenges

**Ignoring Deeper Feelings**: Not all feelings can be solved like a puzzle. Sometimes, a Gemini has to sit with sadness or anger for a bit before it starts to ease.

**Skipping Empathy**: In trying to fix things logically, they might forget that simply acknowledging a feeling (in themselves or others) can be important, too.

## Quick Shifts and Surprises

A common observation is how fast Geminis might switch from one emotion to another. One moment, they could be joking around; the next, they could be irritated or quiet. People close to Geminis sometimes wonder if these mood changes mean Geminis are "fake" or not taking things seriously, but that is not necessarily the case.

### Possible Reasons

**New Information**: Hearing a single piece of news can change a Gemini's outlook. Their mind grabs onto the news, resulting in a new feeling.

**High Reactivity**: Some Geminis are simply sensitive to events around them, reacting more quickly than other signs might.

**Thirst for Novelty**: Emotional variety can feel more interesting to them than staying in one mood for a long stretch, so they lean into changes.

These quick changes can be a challenge in relationships, because friends or family might struggle to keep up. However, if others understand this trait, they might see that each shift reflects a real response to what is on the Gemini's mind at the moment.

## Handling Worry and Stress

Because Geminis think a lot, they can be prone to worry or stress, especially if they get trapped in a loop of overthinking. Maybe they have too many tasks, or they have a conflict with a friend and cannot stop replaying it in their head. This can lead to sleepless nights or a restless feeling they cannot shake.

### Suggestions for Coping

**Writing It Down**: A Gemini can jot down worries or concerns in a notebook or phone note. This step often makes the worries feel more manageable.

**Talking It Out**: Chatting with someone trusted—like a friend, sibling, or counselor—can help sort out which worries are real threats and which are unlikely.

**Taking Mental Breaks**: Doing something creative, like drawing or playing an instrument, can break the worry cycle and give a Gemini's mind a rest.

By combining these methods, Geminis can approach their anxious feelings more calmly, rather than spinning into bigger stress.

## Deeper Feelings Beneath the Surface

Though Geminis can seem playful and talk-focused, they do have depths to their emotions. Sometimes, they hide heavier feelings—like heartbreak or disappointment—behind humor or by switching to a fresh topic. This might leave others thinking the Gemini is not affected by sadness or hurt, but that is not true.

**Why Geminis Might Hide Deeper Feelings**

**Discomfort with Silence**: Sitting quietly with sadness feels unfamiliar if they are used to talking through everything.

**Desire to Stay Positive**: They might worry about bringing other people's mood down if they reveal serious struggles.

**Fear of Being Judged**: Not all Geminis want others to see them as "weak," so they might cover up with jokes or by changing the subject.

However, when Geminis do allow themselves to acknowledge these heavier emotions, they can learn a lot about themselves. They might realize that it is okay to be upset sometimes, and that opening up to close friends or family about sadness can bring genuine support.

## Emotional Connection with Others

Geminis can form close bonds with people who appreciate both their mental side and their emotional side. Because Geminis can chat so easily, they might connect through shared thoughts before revealing deeper feelings. Over time, these conversations can lead to real closeness if both parties are willing to open up.

**Ways Geminis Show They Care**

**Sending Random Messages**: A Gemini might text a friend or family member out of the blue with a funny story, simply to brighten their day.

**Offering Advice**: They share suggestions or solutions, trying to help the other person feel better.

**Making Time**: Despite their many interests, when a Gemini truly cares, they will often drop what they are doing to be there for someone who needs them.

In bigger emotional moments—like if a friend is grieving—Geminis might feel unsure how to respond. They may try cheering the friend up or offering logical tips. Sometimes, just sitting quietly with a friend and saying, "I'm here for you," works better. Balancing their natural talkative nature with calm empathy can strengthen that bond.

## Anger and Frustration in Geminis

Geminis are not always cheerful. They can become angry or annoyed if they feel misunderstood, trapped, or if they see unfairness. Their anger might come out as sharp words or sarcastic remarks. Sometimes, they calm down quickly after letting out frustration, while the other person is left feeling confused or upset.

### What Triggers Gemini Anger

**Feeling Ignored**: If they are trying to explain something and believe nobody is listening, they can get irritated.

**Being Controlled**: Strict rules that do not make sense to them can light a spark of rebellion.

**Seeing Illogical Behavior**: Geminis prize reason in many areas, so if they see actions that seem illogical, they might speak up strongly.

### Tips for Calming Down

**Step Away**: A brief walk or quiet moment can prevent saying something mean in the heat of the moment.

**Use "I" Statements**: Instead of blaming others, a Gemini can say, "I feel upset because…" which often leads to better understanding.

**Listen to the Other Side**: A short talk with the other person—if done calmly—might reveal a middle ground.

## Joy and Excitement

On the positive side, Geminis can be full of joy when something excites them. They might smile wide, talk rapidly about whatever is thrilling them, or invite others to join in their excitement. This can be contagious—friends and family might find themselves feeling happier simply because the Gemini's enthusiasm is so bright.

**Examples of Things That Spark Gemini Joy**

**Learning Something New**: Discovering a cool science fact or a fun word puzzle can light them up.

**Social Events**: A party or group gathering gives them the chance to chat with lots of different people.

**Creative Projects**: Starting an art piece, writing a short story, or trying a new skill can bring them a fresh wave of excitement.

When a Gemini is truly happy, they might share that happiness with everyone around. They may be the friend who organizes a small get-together or the family member who cracks funny jokes during dinner. However, as with any emotion, this excitement can switch if something else grabs their attention, making them seem like they bounce around from one happy spark to another.

## Dealing with Disappointment

Life does not always meet Gemini's high expectations. When hopes are dashed—like missing out on a spot in a club, losing a contest, or having a plan fall through—Geminis can feel a strong sense of letdown. However, they often move past disappointment faster than some other signs, because they look for something new to pour their energy into.

### How Geminis Might Handle Disappointment

**Quick Diversion**: They might jump into a different hobby, idea, or conversation. This can be good because it keeps them from dwelling on negative thoughts, but it can also mean they never fully process the loss.

**Explaining It Away**: Geminis may talk about what happened in detail, analyzing the reasons things went wrong. If it helps them learn a lesson, this can be healthy. If it becomes obsessive, it might keep the sadness alive.

**Seeking Support**: A chat with a sibling, parent, or close friend can help them realize that disappointment is normal and they are not alone.

Over time, Geminis tend to bounce back. Their curiosity naturally pushes them toward new opportunities.

## Sensitivity Behind the Humor

Geminis often use humor as a shield. They might make a joke right when the mood gets too heavy, or tease someone lightly instead of showing that they feel sad. But this does not mean they are not sensitive. In fact, many Geminis can be quite sensitive to criticism or negative feedback—perhaps more than they let on.

### Signs a Gemini Is Hiding Sensitivity

**Sudden Laughter**: They laugh off a serious remark instead of addressing how it affected them.

**Topic Change**: They rapidly shift to a new subject whenever personal feelings come up.

**Overstating Their Calm**: They say, "I'm totally fine," in a way that feels forced.

For friends or family who notice these signs, a gentle approach can help. Asking, "Are you sure you're okay? You can talk to me if you need to," might open the door. Still, Geminis may need time to feel comfortable revealing deeper hurt.

## Emotional Burnout

Because Geminis run on mental stimulation, they can push themselves to keep going, even when they are emotionally tired. Over time, they might reach burnout—where they feel numb, unmotivated, or just drained. This can happen if they have taken on too many tasks, juggled too many social relationships, or tried to keep their mood up without rest.

**Warning Signs**

**Lack of Interest**: They suddenly find everything boring, which is unusual for a curious Gemini.

**Irritability**: Small things set them off, or they snap at loved ones.

**Desire to Hide**: Instead of being chatty, they might withdraw, not returning texts or calls.

**Ways to Recover**

**Intentional Quiet Time**: Even if it feels strange at first, scheduling restful moments—reading alone, taking a peaceful walk—can help.

**Cutting Back**: Dropping one or two activities can free up mental space.

**Asking for Help**: If chores or tasks feel overwhelming, delegating or seeking help from family members or friends can lighten the load.

## Empathy Toward Friends and Family

Geminis may show empathy in their own style. Rather than sitting silently in sorrow with someone, they might try to cheer them up or solve their problems. Still, they do have the ability to understand and share in others' feelings—though they might express it through conversation more than through quiet comfort.

### How Geminis Demonstrate Empathy

**Offering Solutions**: "I'm sorry this happened. Maybe you can try this approach."

**Shifting the Mood**: If a friend is stuck in sadness, a Gemini might bring them a funny video or story to lift their spirit.

**Staying in Touch**: They might check in with someone daily (through texts or quick calls) if they know the person is going through a tough time.

It is good for Geminis to remember that while positivity can help, some people need time to grieve or feel upset. In those cases, simply listening can be more supportive than trying to fix the situation right away.

## Boosting Self-Esteem

A Gemini's active mind might mean they sometimes doubt themselves. They can feel confident one minute and unsure the next, especially if they compare themselves to others who seem more focused on one path. Building self-esteem can help Geminis stay steady emotionally.

**Tips**

**Positive Self-Talk**: Replace thoughts like "I'm not good at anything" with "I'm learning to improve each day."

**Try New Experiences Wisely**: Exploring new interests is great, but being mindful not to overextend can help them see the progress they make in chosen areas.

By recognizing what they do well, Geminis can keep negative self-talk in check and remain happier overall.

## The Role of Creativity in Emotional Life

Many Geminis have a creative streak, whether it is writing, music, art, or inventive ideas. Creativity can serve as an emotional outlet. A Gemini who feels stressed can channel that energy into writing a short story or sketching a picture.

**Why This Helps**

**Expression Without Words**: While Geminis love words, sometimes painting or playing an instrument can release emotions that are hard to articulate.

**Distraction That Heals**: Focusing on a creative project can give the mind a break from stress or worry.

**Sense of Achievement**: Finishing a creative piece can boost mood and self-esteem.

## Shyness vs. Outgoing Behavior

Though many Geminis are described as outgoing, not all are the life of the party. Some might be more reserved in large groups, while still talking a lot in small circles or one-on-one. Emotions can influence whether a Gemini seems shy or outgoing on any given day.

**In Shy Mode**: They might observe the room before jumping into conversations. Their mind might still be busy, but they are choosing not to share as much.

**In Outgoing Mode**: They could chat up strangers, tell jokes, and spark group conversations.

**Switching**: A single event—like receiving surprising news—can push them from one mode to the other in minutes.

Recognizing this can help others see that Gemini behavior is not always predictable, and a usually chatty Gemini might have quieter times depending on emotional factors.

## Building Emotional Resilience

Emotional resilience is the ability to bounce back from setbacks or stress. Geminis have a natural advantage here because of their flexibility and willingness to move on to new ideas. However, true resilience also involves learning from tough emotions, not just avoiding them.

**Ways to Strengthen Resilience**

**Reflect on Lessons**: After a disappointment or conflict, take a moment to think about what could be learned.

**Practice Self-Forgiveness**: If a Gemini regrets something they said in anger, they can offer themselves understanding and decide how to handle it better next time.

**Stay Open to Emotions**: Rather than skipping over sadness or frustration, they can acknowledge it, process it, and then move forward.

## Comfort in Changing Environments

A Gemini's love for change can affect their emotions in new surroundings—like moving to a new city or school. In many cases, they might adapt quickly because they see it as an adventure. However, they can also feel emotional if they must leave old friends or routines behind.

**Adjusting to Change**

**Positive Curiosity**: Exploring the new place helps Geminis get excited, easing any sadness about leaving the old.

**Staying in Touch**: They can keep relationships from their previous home alive through calls, messages, or occasional visits.

**Allowing Time to Grieve**: Even if they are curious about the new setting, it is natural to feel some sadness about what they left. Acknowledging this sadness can help them move forward in a healthy way.

## Romantic Feelings

In situations involving romantic crushes or relationships, Geminis might swing between intense excitement and a more casual stance. They can show big enthusiasm if someone captures their interest, chatting for hours and trying to learn all about that person. However, if the interest fades or they find the person does not match their curiosity, they can shift gears quickly.

## Potential Issues

**Fear of Boredom**: A Gemini might worry that a relationship will become too routine, prompting them to seek variety.

**Communication Overload**: They might text or talk with the person constantly, which can be overwhelming if the other person needs more personal space.

When balanced, a Gemini's ability to communicate can make them caring and fun as a partner, sharing jokes, ideas, and adventures. They just need to remember to slow down and check in on deeper emotional bonds now and then.

## Overcoming Emotional Walls

Sometimes, Geminis build emotional walls for protection. They might keep the conversation light, rarely admitting fears or insecurities, so they will not appear vulnerable. Over time, this can cause them to feel disconnected from deeper relationships.

### Breaking Down the Walls

**Start Small**: Sharing a little personal worry with a close friend or family member can be a first step.

**Notice Safe People**: If someone has proven themselves trustworthy, a Gemini can try opening up more.

**Accept Imperfection**: Admitting they have problems or flaws does not make them less bright or fun. It makes them human.

## Mindfulness and Emotional Awareness

Mindfulness is the act of noticing thoughts and feelings without instantly reacting. Because Geminis have racing minds, practicing mindfulness can help them handle emotions with more calm.

**Simple Ways to Practice**

**Breathing Exercises**: Taking a few slow, deep breaths when they feel an emotion coming on—whether excitement or anger—can slow things down.

**Emotion Check-Ins**: A Gemini could pause throughout the day and ask, "What am I feeling right now? How strong is it?"

**Observing Thoughts**: Instead of following every thought, they can observe them like passing clouds. This gives them a moment to decide how to respond rather than reacting without thinking.

## Asking for Support

Geminis might hesitate to ask for help if they believe they can solve everything through their own logic or quick thinking. Yet there are times when reaching out is the best path. Whether they talk to a guidance counselor, a parent, or a friend, sharing deeper worries can lift a huge weight.

**Why This Matters**

**Stops Isolation**: Keeping tough feelings hidden can make a Gemini feel alone, which often worsens emotional issues.

**Real Solutions**: Others might have ideas or perspectives the Gemini has not considered.

**Emotional Validation**: Simply having someone say, "I understand how you feel," can bring relief.

# Laughing Through Stress

Geminis often use laughter to get through stressful times. They might crack jokes about an upcoming test or poke fun at a tense situation. Laughter can indeed lessen stress and help them (and those around them) feel more at ease. But it can also mask the need for genuine help or a calmer conversation.

**Healthy vs. Unhealthy Laughter**

**Healthy**: Sharing a silly story to lighten the mood before solving a problem is often helpful.

**Unhealthy**: Laughing nonstop to avoid admitting serious stress can prevent them from properly handling the source of the stress.

# Finding Balance in Emotions

The biggest emotional challenge for many Geminis is balance. They can swing between extremes: overly cheerful or deeply worried, highly social or suddenly withdrawn. Learning to identify early signs of an oncoming emotional swing might help them moderate it.

**Practical Steps**

**Track Patterns**: They could keep a short journal, noting the day's main moods and triggers. Over time, patterns might emerge—like feeling irritated after not sleeping well, or feeling anxious before a big event.

**Plan for Swings**: If they know a stressful event is coming, they can schedule coping strategies (like a relaxing activity) right afterward.

**Seek Feedback**: Asking friends or family to kindly mention if they notice the Gemini seems overly tense or anxious can provide a helpful outside perspective.

# CHAPTER 10: MAKING PLANS WITH GEMINI

Geminis are often adventurous thinkers who like to explore a range of ideas. When it comes to making plans—whether for a weekend activity, a family trip, or a long-term project—they tend to bring excitement, curiosity, and a flair for the unexpected. Yet planning can also reveal some of Gemini's common challenges, like difficulty settling on one choice or quickly shifting course if a new option seems more fun.

In this chapter, we will look at how Geminis go about making plans, how they communicate those plans to others, and why they might change directions at the last minute. We will also give simple tips on how Geminis can stick with their decisions while still keeping things interesting. By understanding a Gemini's approach to planning, friends and family can better enjoy the surprises and fun that this sign brings—without losing track of what everyone needs to do.

## The Excitement of Planning New Things

For Geminis, making plans can be energizing. If they are choosing where to go for a day trip or deciding on a new hobby, they often light up with ideas. They might research places to visit, watch videos, read reviews, or ask around to gather facts. Their heads can fill up with everything from the location's history to what snacks might be available.

### Why Geminis Enjoy This

**Curiosity**: Planning is a chance to learn about something new, whether it is a city, a type of event, or a special activity.

**Conversation**: Geminis love discussing possibilities with friends or family, tossing around ideas for what to do.

**Boost of Energy**: The feeling of stepping into the unknown can feel like a mini-adventure, which Geminis often crave.

In this excitement, however, Geminis might not always think about practical details—like costs, travel times, or how the plan fits with everyone's schedules.

## Spontaneous vs. Detailed Planning

Some Geminis prefer spontaneous decisions, deciding in the moment what to do. Others might enjoy making a detailed plan, then flipping parts of it if something better arises. The difference often depends on a Gemini's personal habits and life situation.

**Spontaneous Geminis**

**Pros**: Flexible, open to last-minute invitations, can turn a dull afternoon into something fun on a whim.

**Cons**: Might forget to check if others are free, or realize too late that they lack the time or resources needed.

**Detailed-Plan Geminis**

**Pros**: Can outline multiple steps, foresee issues, and keep track of the smaller details.

**Cons**: May become bored if the plan is locked in too soon, leading them to change it anyway.

No matter which style they lean toward, Geminis can sometimes strike a balance: plan a rough outline but remain flexible about specifics.

## Collaborating with Others

When Geminis make plans with a group—like friends, classmates, or family—they often handle the role of idea-generator. They propose different places to visit, new games to play, or creative ways to spend time together. However, not everyone can keep up with their quick shifts and multiple suggestions.

**Tips for Effective Collaboration**

**Narrow the Options**: If a Gemini throws out ten ideas, it might overwhelm the group. Sharing two or three strong options is usually enough to start.

**Listen to Responses**: After presenting ideas, Geminis should pause and let others say what they think.

**Aim for Agreement**: Geminis can use their communication skills to find a middle ground if the group is divided.

If the group decides on something, the Gemini can help by writing down the plan or sending a group message so everyone stays on the same page.

## Why Plans Might Change Suddenly

It is common for Gemini-led plans to switch at the last minute. They might promise a friend, "We'll meet at this cafe on Saturday," then later suggest another spot because they found a new cafe that has live music. For people who love routine, this can be frustrating.

**Possible Reasons**

**New Discoveries**: Geminis might find something they think is more interesting.

**Fear of Missing Out**: They worry the original plan might not be as exciting as the new option.

**Restlessness**: Sticking to one decision can feel limiting if something else pops up.

While spontaneity can keep life lively, too many sudden changes can cause confusion. Geminis may want to confirm if others are okay with the shift or if they have their hearts set on the original plan.

## Handling Long-Term Goals

Geminis often thrive on short-term ideas. However, bigger goals—like finishing a lengthy project or saving money for an expensive purchase—can require sustained focus, which might be hard for them. They may have the initial excitement to set the goal, but lose interest or switch aims when a new prospect arises.

**Strategies to Stay on Track**

**Break It Into Parts**: Divide a big goal into smaller, manageable tasks, so each step feels fresh and doable.

**Set Reminders**: Using a calendar or phone alerts can keep them aware of upcoming deadlines.

**Share the Plan**: Telling a friend or family member helps Geminis stick to the goal. That person can check in and encourage them to keep going.

## Travel Plans and Adventures

When it comes to traveling, Geminis can be top-notch planners in some ways. They might research fun attractions, unusual local spots, or hidden gems. They can also pick up on details like train schedules or interesting routes. However, they might also get bored if each day's itinerary is too strict.

**Gemini Travel Style**

**Seeking Variety**: They might want to visit a museum in the morning, have lunch at a local café, then hike in the afternoon, followed by a music show at night.

**Adapting to Changes**: If a train is canceled or a site is closed, they are likely to pivot quickly to something else.

**Possible Pitfall**: Overloading the schedule with too many stops, which can leave everyone exhausted.

Friends and family traveling with a Gemini might enjoy a more dynamic trip, but they should also gently remind the Gemini to include rest and not cram in every single idea.

## Planning Social Events

Geminis often have a wide circle of friends. If they try to plan a party or gathering, they might invite people from different groups. This can create a colorful event, full of varied interests. Still, mixing groups also needs organization.

**Thoughts for Gemini Hosts**

**Set a Clear Time and Place**: Because Geminis can forget details when excited, they should pick a date, location, and start time that everyone knows.

**Offer a Loose Structure**: Maybe plan one main activity (like a board game or a group challenge) but leave space for everyone to chat and mingle

**Be Ready for Changes**: If certain guests show up late or bring extra friends, a Gemini usually handles that well, as they are flexible. However, they should keep track so the event does not become chaotic.

When the event ends, a Gemini might quickly move on to the next idea for another gathering if it felt successful. If it had issues, they might be the first to say, "Let's try something different next time," rather than dwelling on what went wrong.

## Family Plans and Responsibilities

At home, family members might rely on a Gemini to help plan birthdays, weekend outings, or holiday get-togethers. While Geminis excel at generating ideas, a parent or sibling might worry if the plans will stick.

**Ways to Support Family Planning**

**Agree on a General Theme**: Let the Gemini pick a theme or location.

**Share Tasks**: If the plan is complex, assign some chores to the Gemini (like calling a venue) and some to others (like preparing food or shopping).

**Confirm Before Finalizing**: The family should double-check details with the Gemini a few days before the event to see if any last-minute changes cropped up.

## School or Work Projects

In a school or work context, Geminis might find themselves leading or contributing to projects that need coordination. Their imaginative input can boost the quality of the final result, but they might also get restless with long timelines.

**Strength**: They can brainstorm creative angles, design interesting presentations, and keep the group inspired.

**Weakness**: If the project requires months of careful planning, Geminis can drift, possibly missing deadlines or forgetting details.

### Helpful Steps

**Outline Each Phase**: Write a timeline of tasks, so the Gemini can see a structure.

**Update Meetings**: Regular check-ins let the Gemini share new ideas while ensuring the group stays on the path.

## Personal Schedules

On a day-to-day basis, Geminis might keep mental schedules. They could think, "I'll do homework at 4 PM, meet a friend at 5 PM, and practice an instrument at 6 PM." But because they are flexible, these times can slide around. If something more interesting appears, they might drop the original plan.

**Possible Problems**

**Overbooking**: They say yes to multiple appointments, then realize there is no way to attend them all.

**Rushing**: They leave tasks unfinished as they hurry to the next item on the list.

**Forgetting Commitments**: If it is not written down, they might simply forget.

**Solutions**

**Calendar Apps**: Many Geminis find success with a calendar app that sends reminders.

**Prioritizing**: If two plans clash, they can decide which is more important and politely decline the other.

**Allowing Buffer Time**: Building in small gaps between activities helps them handle delays or last-minute changes without stress.

# Handling Disagreements About Plans

Sometimes, friends or family might want a predictable schedule, but a Gemini might prefer a flexible approach. This can cause disagreements. For instance, if someone wants to book tickets for a show well in advance, but the Gemini says, "Let's wait and see how we feel that day," there can be tension.

**Conflict Resolution**

**Compromise**: Book tickets for the main event but leave the rest of the day open-ended.

**Communication**: Both sides explain their reasons. If someone absolutely needs advance notice, the Gemini should respect that. If the Gemini wants freedom, maybe they can keep a portion of the day free.

**Respect**: Remember that differences in planning style are not personal attacks; it is just how each person's mind works.

## Motivation Peaks and Valleys

A Gemini might be super motivated when a plan first forms. They could spend hours talking about it, researching, and even writing down steps. But after a short time, they might lose that spark, especially if the plan becomes routine.

### Recognizing the Cycle

**Peak**: Ideas flow, excitement is high, lots of chatter and research.

**Dip**: The novelty fades. If no new angle is introduced, the Gemini might drop the plan.

**Regain Interest**: If something about the plan changes or evolves, the Gemini can become excited again.

Friends and family who understand this cycle can help by adding new details or tasks that revive the Gemini's curiosity. For example, if it is a garden project, let the Gemini experiment with an unusual plant or design, so each phase feels fresh.

## The Temptation of Multiple Options

Geminis can struggle when choosing between different plans. They might say, "I want to go hiking, but I also want to see that new exhibit." The result is that they may jump between these two ideas, feeling unsure which one to settle on.

### Coping Tactics

**Plan Two Separate Days**: If it is possible, do one activity this week and the other next week.

**Combine Them If Feasible**: If the hike is in the morning and the exhibit is in the afternoon, that might work—but only if it is realistic in terms of time and location.

**Ask for Input**: Sometimes, letting a friend or family member pick can break the decision deadlock.

**Accept That One Option Must Be Let Go**: Geminis can remind themselves that missing one plan is not the end of the world.

## Surprise vs. Certainty

Geminis often like surprising others with fun twists in plans, like a secret stop at a bakery or an unexpected puzzle game at a party. Surprises can add excitement, but certain people may prefer to know everything ahead of time.

### Balancing Surprises

**Share the Basics**: Tell people the core plan so they can prepare (like what time to arrive, what to wear).

**Keep a Small Twist**: Hide one playful element, such as a silly game or a treat, to reveal during the outing.

## Delegating Responsibilities

If a plan involves multiple tasks (booking tickets, preparing food, inviting guests), Geminis might try to do it all at once because they think they can handle it. But if they lose focus or get distracted, important steps might slip through the cracks.

### How to Delegate

**List All Tasks**: Write down everything the plan requires.

**Assign Tasks Clearly**: If friends or family are helping, give each person a specific job.

**Follow Up**: A quick check ensures each person is on track. This also helps the Gemini avoid last-minute panic.

## Handling Cost and Practical Details

Geminis might be more concerned with how fun or interesting a plan sounds than with the cost or logistics. This can lead to trouble if they plan something beyond their budget or forget practical limits.

### Staying Realistic

**Set a Budget**: If money is tight, decide how much can be spent beforehand.

**Check Resources**: If the plan requires certain tools or materials, see what is actually available.

**Allow for Travel Time**: Geminis might forget that traveling can eat up hours, so they should double-check routes and times.

## Planning for Special Occasions

If a Gemini is in charge of a bigger event—like a group gift-giving, a family feast, or a themed party—they can excel at brainstorming unique ideas. They might think of creative decorations or unusual activities. The challenge is turning these ideas into a workable plan.

### Tips for Larger Events

**Make a Timeline**: Mark when each step has to be done (invites sent, items bought, tasks assigned).

**Ask for Creative Input**: Geminis are happy to gather suggestions from others, but they should not let it spiral into 50 different half-formed plans.

**Simplify**: If the plan becomes too complicated, cut back to the strongest elements.

# Keeping Promises

One frequent complaint about Geminis is that they make big promises about plans but do not always follow through. They might say, "I'll definitely organize that club outing!" and then get sidetracked. This can make friends or coworkers hesitate to rely on them.

**Building Reliability**

**Under-Promise, Over-Deliver**: Instead of promising a big plan, a Gemini can start smaller. If they succeed, they can add more.

**Set Alarms or Notes**: Use phone reminders or sticky notes to remember key tasks.

**Clear Communication**: If something truly cannot be done, speak up early instead of vanishing from the responsibility.

Over time, showing follow-through can improve a Gemini's reputation as a fun but also dependable planner.

# Changing Plans When Necessary

Sometimes, events outside anyone's control—like bad weather, closed venues, or unexpected emergencies—can force a change in plans. Geminis usually adapt well to these situations, often better than other signs, because they thrive on shifting gears.

**How Geminis Can Use Their Strength Here**

**Instant Brainstorming**: They can propose a new plan right away, which calms any panic in the group.

**Positive Attitude**: Their excitement about the new option can be contagious, making others feel less disappointed.

**Caution**: Make sure the new plan is truly realistic, rather than just the first wild idea that comes to mind.

## Dealing with Mixed Personalities in a Group

If a group includes both free-spirited members and those who like strict planning, conflicts can arise. Geminis often fall on the flexible side, but not always. They can help mediate if they understand both viewpoints.

### Approach

**Address Concerns**: Ask the structured person, "What do you need to feel comfortable?" and the flexible person, "What do you want to leave open?"

**Create a Hybrid Plan**: Outline a schedule but include built-in times where the group can pick from a few options or go with the flow.

**Use Clear Language**: Geminis can use their communication ability to ensure everyone feels heard and included.

## Personal Hobbies and Plans

Outside of group settings, Geminis often have personal hobbies or dreams they want to pursue—like learning a language, mastering a game, or starting a blog. They might make a plan to practice daily or reach certain milestones.

**Enthusiasm Launch**: The Gemini begins strong, possibly telling everyone about their goal.

**Dip in Interest**: After a few weeks, the routine can become boring.

**Ways to Keep Going**:

**Switch Methods**: If they are learning a language, they can try different apps or find a conversation partner instead of using only a textbook.

**Track Progress**: Writing down small improvements can keep their excitement alive.

**Reward System**: After a set amount of practice, they treat themselves to something they enjoy (like a favorite snack or a short break).

## Communication When Plans Are Cancelled

Sometimes, a Gemini might realize they cannot or do not want to continue with a plan. Letting others know promptly is crucial, rather than just disappearing. If they change their mind at the last minute, explaining it politely helps avoid hurt feelings.

**What to Say**

**Apologize**: "I'm really sorry, but I have to cancel our plan."

**Give a Brief Reason**: "Something came up at home," or "I overcommitted my schedule."

**Suggest Another Time** (if they genuinely want to reschedule): "Could we try next week?"

Being honest is better than leaving others in confusion, which can damage trust.

## Planning for Personal Well-Being

Geminis might focus on external plans—like social events or group outings—and overlook personal well-being plans. For instance, they might forget to schedule regular rest, exercise, or peaceful breaks in a hectic week.

**Self-Care Planning**

**Daily Reminders**: Set a reminder to do something calming, like stretching or reading for fun.

**Check Emotional State**: If the Gemini notices they are feeling run-down, they can plan a quiet evening instead of going out again.

**Balance**: A well-planned personal schedule that includes downtime helps Geminis stay energetic and prevents burnout.

## Reflections on Completed Plans

After a plan wraps up—be it a trip, a party, or a finished project—Geminis might sprint to the next idea without pausing. But reflecting on what went well and what could have been better can improve future planning.

**Reflection Questions**

**What Did I Enjoy Most?** This helps Geminis spot patterns in what truly excites them.

**What Went Wrong (If Anything)?** Understanding mistakes can help them avoid repeats, like double-booking or forgetting a crucial step.

**Did Everyone Involved Have Fun?** Checking how friends or family felt about the plan can strengthen relationships.

Taking a short time for reflection can turn each planning experience into a stepping stone for better ones ahead.

## Conclusion

Making plans with a Gemini can be a lively experience. Their curious mind, love of novelty, and skill with words often lead to exciting ideas that nobody else would have thought of. Whether it is a casual hangout with friends or a big family event, Geminis bring energy and a sense of exploration to the table. However, they also face the challenge of staying on track, avoiding sudden last-minute changes, and managing the practical side of things like budgets and timelines.

When Geminis learn to balance their spontaneity with organization, they can become excellent planners. They just need to keep a few tools handy—like a calendar, a system for breaking tasks down, and a willingness to listen to what others need. Friends, family, and colleagues who understand a Gemini's style can help shape ideas into workable plans while still leaving room for the surprises that make any outing memorable. In the end, planning with a Gemini can be a fun and refreshing process, as long as everyone stays open to the twists and turns that might pop up along the way.

# CHAPTER 11: GEMINI AND WORK LIFE

Geminis often show a lively and flexible style in many areas of life, including the world of work. Whether they are managing tasks in an office or juggling projects on a team, they tend to bring curiosity and versatility to their roles. Yet, just as with other parts of life, Geminis may run into some challenges at work if they are not careful. In this chapter, we will look at what makes Geminis tick in a job setting, the kinds of careers that might interest them, the skills they bring to the table, and how they can handle issues that pop up. We will also discuss how Geminis relate to coworkers, supervisors, and any group they work with. By understanding how Geminis work best, they can shape a work life that plays to their strengths while staying aware of potential pitfalls.

## The Appeal of Variety

Many Geminis do not thrive if they repeat the same tasks day after day without change. They can lose energy or interest if their job requires doing one thing for many hours straight, with no chance to learn something new. Because their minds are often engaged in more than one idea at a time, Geminis usually enjoy positions that allow them to handle varied tasks, shift gears, and solve new problems.

**Examples of Varied Work:**

- Working in a job that rotates responsibilities each week.
- Serving as a point person for multiple short-term projects.
- Helping different teams or departments as needed, rather than staying in only one role.

Of course, no job is exciting all day, every day. Still, Geminis might seek roles that offer an ongoing mix of tasks. This variety keeps them engaged and taps into their capacity to handle more than one matter at once.

## Communication Strengths

Geminis often have a natural gift for speaking, writing, and explaining topics. In the workplace, this can become a major plus. Whether it is talking with clients, sending emails, giving presentations, or leading a discussion, Geminis can express ideas in a clear and lively way. This can help them stand out in group settings and even earn them a reputation as the person who can chat with almost anyone.

**Ways Geminis Excel Here**:

- **Client Relations**: They might do well dealing with customers or clients, since they can adapt to different personalities and keep the conversation flowing.

- **Presentations**: When asked to share new proposals or explain data, Geminis can create a vivid and engaging talk.

- **Team Building**: They may be skilled at encouraging coworkers to share ideas, or smoothing over rough spots in group chats.

Because of their comfort with language, many Geminis find success in roles that require an outgoing nature or the ability to put ideas into words. However, they should also be aware that sometimes they might talk so much that they forget to listen thoroughly to what others say.

## Quick Learners

Another trait Geminis bring to work is the ability to pick up new information quickly. Their minds thrive on input and can absorb facts and methods faster than some others might. This can make them excellent at training sessions, adapting to fresh technology, or shifting to a new project on short notice. Supervisors often appreciate how Geminis can handle a fast-paced environment or a sudden change in plan without much fuss.

**Examples of Quick Learning:**

**Tech Upgrades:** If the company updates its software, a Gemini might master its basic functions promptly and then show colleagues how it works.

**New Procedures:** If a new process is introduced, Geminis may adapt faster than most, becoming comfortable sooner.

**Taking Over Tasks:** If a coworker leaves or gets sick, Geminis could step in and figure out the role with limited guidance, at least for the short term.

That said, it is important for Geminis to keep this strength balanced. If they leap from learning one thing to the next without following through on the first, that can lead to half-finished tasks.

## Handling Routine Tasks

Even in jobs that provide variety, there are often some routine chores that just need to be done. This might be filing forms, entering data, running standard checks, or other predictable tasks. Geminis might find these parts of the job boring if they do not see any mental challenge. Yet, ignoring these tasks is not an option if they are essential to the role.

**Possible Solutions:**

**Make It Interesting:** Turn it into a short game by timing how long it takes, or by doing it while listening to background music (if allowed).

**Use Quick Bursts:** Instead of letting routine tasks accumulate, do them in brief, focused periods. This can help Geminis avoid feeling stuck.

**Ask for a Switch:** If the workload can be shared, maybe a coworker who prefers routine tasks can trade duties with the Gemini, who might take on more creative tasks in return.

By being proactive and creative, Geminis can manage routine work without letting it drain all their energy.

## Common Career Paths

Because Geminis often excel at communication, learning, and variety, there are some areas of work where they might feel especially at home. Of course, Geminis can be found in almost any field, but certain areas tend to mesh well with their traits:

**Media and Journalism**: Writing, interviewing, reporting news, or hosting shows can suit Geminis who love to talk and find out what is new.

**Public Relations or Marketing**: These roles let them connect with many people, create messages, and switch projects often.

**Teaching or Training**: Explaining ideas to students or coworkers can be a way for Geminis to use their verbal gifts. They can make lessons engaging, as long as they keep themselves organized.

**Sales and Customer Service**: These jobs involve chatting with new folks frequently, matching needs to solutions, and adapting to different personalities.

**Tech and Innovation**: Geminis who love gadgets and trends might do well in a fast-moving tech space, where new products appear all the time.

**Events or Hospitality**: Planning and hosting different functions can appeal to Geminis who enjoy bringing people together and solving problems on the fly.

Of course, these are not the only places a Gemini can thrive. The key is often finding a position that plays to their love of change, mental flexibility, and communication skills.

## Challenges with Deadlines

In a work setting, Geminis might struggle at times with deadlines, especially if the project is long or the finishing steps are tedious. They might work quickly and well at first, then slow down when excitement fades. This can leave them rushing at the last moment or even missing a due date.

**How to Cope**:

**Plan in Blocks**: Schedule tasks in smaller parts, each with its own mini-deadline.

**Set Reminders**: Use a calendar or phone alerts so the final due date does not sneak up unexpectedly.

**Reward System**: Give themselves a small treat or break whenever they complete a stage. This keeps motivation higher over time.

When Geminis take control of their approach to deadlines, they can avoid the stress that comes with last-minute scrambles.

## Team Dynamics

Geminis can bring humor and lively chats to a team, helping the group stay upbeat. They often sense how each person can contribute. However, some coworkers might find a Gemini's fast speech or quick changes confusing if they are not prepared.

**Tips for Team Harmony**:

**Listen Actively**: Geminis should remind themselves to let others finish their thoughts fully.

**Be Clear**: If they propose a new idea halfway through a project, they should explain exactly why it helps rather than just dumping it on the group.

**Follow Agreed Plans**: Once the team decides on a direction, it is important that the Gemini does not suddenly change it again without discussing.

By balancing their natural desire for new ideas with respect for the team's process, Geminis can become valued team members who keep projects fresh and moving forward.

## Working Under Different Types of Bosses

Geminis might thrive or struggle depending on their supervisor's style:

**Boss Who Encourages Freedom**: If the manager is open-minded and allows employees to approach tasks in their own way, a Gemini can shine. They will enjoy the flexibility and can produce strong results.

**Boss Who Is Strict and Rigid**: This can be tough for Geminis, who may feel stifled if every detail is micro-managed. They might resist rules that do not seem logical, creating tension.

**Boss Who Values Communication**: This is usually ideal, because Geminis can talk openly, show their ideas, and get feedback in a timely way.

No matter the style, Geminis who practice respect and adaptability can often find ways to work with different personalities. If they do run into clashes, calm discussions or seeking small compromises might help.

## Stress Management

Work can be stressful for anyone, and Geminis can feel the strain if they have too many tasks at once or if they are bored with a slow period. They might respond to stress by chatting with coworkers, shifting tasks frequently, or diving into side projects. But this can be distracting if not managed well.

**Ways to Reduce Stress**:

**Set Realistic Goals**: Avoid saying "yes" to every request if it is not possible to complete them all well.

**Take Short Breaks**: A quick mental reset (like walking for a couple of minutes) can calm a Gemini's busy mind.

**Keep Communication Clear**: If a deadline is not possible, telling the boss sooner rather than later helps avoid last-minute panic.

Finding a healthy mix of challenge and downtime can keep Geminis engaged without leading to burnout.

## Innovation and Fresh Ideas

One reason many workplaces value Geminis is that they bring a steady flow of ideas. They might suggest a new way to organize information, a fresh angle for a marketing strategy, or a smarter approach to scheduling. This creative spark can help a business stay ahead.

**Examples of Gemini-Led Innovation:**

Streamlining how the team shares files, perhaps by introducing a new app or method.

Proposing a social media campaign with a fun twist that captures attention.

Helping coworkers see where a process can be trimmed to save time.

Of course, not every idea will be practical. Geminis benefit from learning which thoughts are truly useful and how to present them in a way that others can understand and support.

## Time-Management Techniques

Because Geminis might switch focus easily, they need effective time-management habits. Otherwise, they risk having multiple half-done tasks. Some strategies include:

**Creating Detailed Lists**: Breaking down each item and checking them off can satisfy the Gemini's mind, giving a sense of progress.

**The "Two-Minute Rule"**: If a small task takes two minutes or less, do it right away instead of adding it to a list. This keeps minor things from piling up.

**Batching Similar Tasks**: If they have several phone calls to make, they can do them in a single session, then move on to something else.

By applying these methods, Geminis can stay more centered and ensure they do not leave tasks unfinished.

## Changing Jobs or Roles

Geminis might feel drawn to switch jobs more often than some other signs. This does not mean they cannot be loyal employees, but if they sense there is no more room to learn or grow, they might start looking elsewhere. As a result, they could have a resume showing various roles, which can be both positive and negative.

**Positive Side**: Broad experiences can show adaptability and a wide range of skills.

**Potential Downside**: Some employers may worry that the Gemini will not stay long-term.

If a Gemini wants to stay in one place, they can look for ways to keep the work feeling fresh, such as asking for new responsibilities, cross-training, or joining committees that help them learn new aspects of the business. This allows them to stay engaged without jumping to another job too soon.

## Remote Work and Gemini Traits

In recent times, many jobs offer remote or flexible work options. A Gemini might enjoy remote work because it allows them to arrange their schedule more freely. They can take short breaks to reset their mind, shift tasks throughout the day, and often have more control over their environment. However, remote work also requires self-discipline.

**Tips for Remote Gemini Workers**:

**Plan a Daily Schedule**: Write down tasks and set times so they do not float from one idea to the next all day.

**Use Video Chats**: They can maintain a sense of connection by talking face-to-face with teammates online.

**Keep a Dedicated Workspace**: Having a specific spot for work can help them stay in "work mode" rather than mixing tasks with personal distractions all day.

If they remain organized, remote work can give Geminis the variety they crave, as they can do different tasks in different parts of the day.

## Handling Office Politics

In many workplaces, there are unofficial rules, cliques, or rivalries. Geminis, being social, might move among different groups easily. They can be good at connecting people who do not usually talk. But there is also a risk that a Gemini who shares too many inside details could get caught in the middle of office drama.

**Advice**:

**Keep Private Matters Private**: If a coworker confides something, do not pass it on in casual conversation.

**Stay Neutral**: If two sides are feuding, it is safer not to pick sides unless it is a work necessity.

**Be Fair**: Treat people with respect. Being known as evenhanded can help a Gemini avoid messy workplace politics.

By using their communication gifts wisely, Geminis can ease tension rather than make it worse.

## Maintaining Motivation Over Time

Many Geminis are motivated by fresh sparks of interest. But work can have slow phases or repetitive periods. Staying motivated might require some effort.

**Ideas for Motivation**:

**Look for Micro-Challenges**: Even if the task is routine, the Gemini can find small goals, like finishing it in a shorter time or discovering a quicker method.

**Ask for Feedback**: Positive words from a boss or coworker can encourage them to keep going. Also, constructive suggestions can lead to new approaches that may re-spark interest.

**Set Personal Targets**: Beyond official goals, Geminis can set personal growth aims, such as learning one new skill each month.

By focusing on improvement and small achievements, Geminis can remain energized, even in less-than-exciting times.

## Conflict Resolution

When conflicts arise at work, Geminis might jump into the discussion, trying to fix it with quick talk. This can help if they listen well and show empathy. But if they move too fast or talk over others, it can aggravate tensions.

**Conflict Tips**:

**Hear Each Person Out**: Geminis can use their curiosity to understand every side.

**Speak Calmly**: Even if the conversation is heated, keeping a level tone can reduce friction.

**Suggest Options**: Because Geminis see multiple viewpoints, they might propose a compromise or a fresh approach that suits everyone.

If used kindly and patiently, a Gemini's communication skills can turn them into a peacemaker in the office.

## Professional Growth

Geminis often look for ways to grow in their field. They might sign up for workshops, online courses, or new certifications that match their interests. This keeps their minds active. Yet, they should ensure they pick courses they can complete rather than signing up for too many and not finishing them.

**Steps to Grow:**

**Choose Relevant Topics**: Focus on skills that can help their current role or open doors for future roles they truly desire.

**Plan Study Time**: Fit learning into their schedule, so they do not fall behind.

**Share Knowledge**: After learning something new, a Gemini might present it to coworkers or create a short guide. This builds their reputation as a helpful resource.

By channeling their love of knowledge into real accomplishments, Geminis can advance at work while staying fulfilled.

## Leading a Team

Some Geminis might step into leadership roles, where they supervise others. They can be enthusiastic leaders who inspire team members with fresh ideas. Their open communication style can build trust, and they are usually willing to hear suggestions. However, they need to watch out for a few pitfalls:

**Overloading the Team with Ideas**: A Gemini leader might constantly propose changes, making it hard for the group to settle on a direction.

**Struggle with Organization**: Leading a team requires careful tracking of tasks, deadlines, and progress. If the Gemini gets scattered, the team might become confused.

**Need for Consistency**: Team members appreciate a leader who is predictable in how they handle rules, feedback, and responsibilities.

By combining their natural enthusiasm with structured planning, Geminis can guide a team successfully and keep morale high.

## Balancing Socializing and Productivity

Geminis tend to be social by nature. While some quick chatting at work can build relationships and keep the environment friendly, they should make sure these conversations do not eat into too much productive time.

**How to Maintain Balance**:

**Set Boundaries**: Know when it is time to work quietly versus when it is acceptable to talk.

**Use Break Times**: Catch up with coworkers during breaks or lunch, so main tasks are not interrupted.

**Read Social Cues**: If a coworker seems busy or stressed, it is better not to start a lighthearted conversation that might distract them.

By keeping an eye on timing, Geminis can enjoy workplace friendships while still meeting their responsibilities.

## Working Alone vs. Working in Groups

Geminis often enjoy group settings because they get to exchange ideas. But some tasks require quiet focus. A Gemini might do well in an office that offers both private spaces for individual tasks and common areas for collaboration.

**Alone Work Tips**:

**Short Bursts**: Break a long solo project into timed segments, with a quick rest after each.

**Background Support**: Some Geminis find it helpful to have soft music or background noise to stay focused.

**Check-Ins**: After finishing a chunk, they might share progress with a coworker or boss, getting feedback that keeps them motivated.

# Adapting to Change

Companies often go through changes—new technology, restructuring, or shifts in strategy. Geminis can handle these transitions better than most, as they are used to adapting. They might even enjoy the fresh energy that comes with change, so long as it does not become too chaotic.

**Tips to Thrive During Change**:

**Stay Informed**: Ask questions, attend any briefings, and read all updates, so no details are missed.

**Offer Help**: Geminis can support coworkers who feel uncertain by explaining changes or sharing tips.

**Suggest Solutions**: If a new system is introduced, Geminis might propose helpful ways to roll it out, using their creative thinking.

Being a positive force during transitions can enhance a Gemini's standing at work.

# Recognition and Encouragement

Geminis often appreciate positive feedback. They can feel energized when a boss or peer recognizes their contributions, whether it is for a creative solution, strong communication, or quick thinking. However, they also want feedback that is honest. Empty praise does not carry much weight. They prefer to hear genuine thanks for real achievements.

**Ways to Seek Encouragement**:

**Show Results**: If they create a new method that saves time or money, they can present the impact to their supervisor or the team.

**Ask for Evaluations**: In a performance review or informal check-in, they can request specific feedback on how to improve.

By supporting each other, Geminis and their coworkers can create a workplace where everyone's contributions are noticed.

## Long-Term Satisfaction

To remain happy in a job for the long run, a Gemini might need ongoing growth opportunities. If their role becomes too predictable or they stop learning, dissatisfaction may arise. They should watch for signs of boredom, such as frequently daydreaming, procrastinating tasks, or feeling restless.

**Renewing Satisfaction**:

**Look for In-House Moves**: Maybe shift to a different department or a slightly different role if possible.

**Discuss with a Mentor or Boss**: A supportive mentor could point them toward fresh projects or training.

**Create Side Projects**: If time allows, they can suggest new initiatives that interest them, adding variety to the routine.

## Conclusion

Geminis in the workplace bring a spirit of curiosity, adaptability, and skilled communication. They often do best in roles that allow for variety and creativity, where they can express new ideas and learn at a quick pace. Whether they are handling client relations, designing innovative strategies, or leading a team, Geminis can make a strong impression by sharing fresh perspectives and connecting well with others.

However, Geminis should keep an eye on a few possible issues, such as losing focus if the work is too repetitive, taking on too many tasks at once, or switching plans too often. Tools like careful scheduling, small goals, and clear communication can help. When Geminis find a balance between their natural flexibility and the steadiness that work sometimes requires, they can experience success and genuine satisfaction on the job.

# CHAPTER 12: GEMINI HOBBIES AND FUN

When Geminis step away from work or studies, they often look for ways to keep their minds busy and their energy flowing. This sign is famous for enjoying a wide range of pastimes—sometimes all at once. From arts and crafts to sports or reading, Geminis typically do not like to stand still for long. They might try an activity one week, then switch to a completely different one the next, driven by curiosity. In this chapter, we will look at what Geminis often enjoy doing for fun, why they can hop between hobbies, and how they might find deeper satisfaction in their free time by balancing novelty with follow-through.

## Loving New Experiences

One thing that sets Geminis apart is their eagerness to try fresh activities. It might be a new board game, a special cooking recipe, or a local workshop on a random topic that intrigues them. Geminis see these as chances to learn and explore something they have not done before. Even if they do not stick with it long, the spark of discovering something new feels exciting.

**Examples of Adventures**:

- A Gemini might sign up for a short dance class, even if they have no plans to continue dancing later.

- They might join a book club just to read unusual authors and discuss with new people.

- They could pick up a musical instrument briefly or try an online class on photography or coding.

The upside is that Geminis rarely get bored, because they always have something fresh to do. The downside is that they might end up with half-used materials or partially learned skills scattered around.

## Social Hobbies

Because Geminis often enjoy communication, many of their pastimes involve people. They might prefer hobbies that allow them to chat, collaborate, or compete in a friendly way. Examples include group sports, board game nights, improvisational theater, or social clubs.

**Group Activities**:

**Trivia Nights**: Geminis might shine at events that let them show off random knowledge.

**Team Sports**: They might try casual soccer, basketball, or other group sports where they can connect with teammates.

**Community Events**: Volunteering or being part of a local group can keep them meeting new folks, learning about different perspectives.

Social hobbies feed Gemini's need for conversation and variety, though they should watch out for overbooking if they sign up for too many gatherings at once.

## Intellectual Pursuits

Even in their free time, Geminis may be drawn to activities that let them think, solve puzzles, or gather facts. Their curiosity does not switch off just because they are relaxing. They might want to read about science, watch documentaries, or play brain-training apps.

**Brainy Pastimes**:

**Crossword Puzzles and Sudoku**: These let Geminis scratch that mental itch of problem-solving.

**Reading Non-Fiction**: Books on history, pop science, or technology can fascinate them.

**Online Forums**: Geminis might enjoy forums or discussion groups where they can debate ideas or learn trivia.

Though these pursuits may look like "work" to some, for Geminis, it is often pure fun to discover new information and share it with others.

## Artistic and Creative Outlets

Many Geminis have a creative streak, enjoying writing, painting, crafting, or making music. They can generate a constant flow of new ideas, which can be turned into short stories, sketches, or songs. Their challenge is often sticking with a project long enough to finish it.

**Artistic Activities**:

**Journaling**: Writing daily notes or short observations can keep their minds engaged.

**Craft Projects**: From making handmade cards to experimenting with pottery, Geminis might dabble in many styles.

**Digital Arts**: Photography, video editing, or graphic design can appeal to the modern, tech-loving side of Gemini.

When Geminis do complete a project, they may feel proud and might share it with friends or on social media for feedback. However, it can be a task to remain motivated if the initial excitement wears off.

## Outdoor Exploration

Not all Geminis love the outdoors, but those who do might find that exploring nature satisfies their desire for variety. They can walk different trails, see changing scenery, and gather fun tidbits along the way, such as noticing interesting rocks or plants. The social aspect can still be there if they hike with a friend or join a local nature club.

**Possible Outdoor Interests**:

**Light Hiking**: Trying new trails or nature parks.

**Urban Walks**: Exploring parts of the city they have not seen before, looking for hidden murals or neat shops.

**Nature Photography**: Combining an interest in technology (camera gear) with a love for new sights.

If a Gemini wants a bit more excitement, they might try mild adventure sports. Still, they should be mindful of safety and plan details carefully, especially if their mind tends to jump from idea to idea.

## Tech and Gadget Hobbies

Many Geminis like to stay current with new technology. Trying out the latest phone, exploring cutting-edge software, or playing with novel gadgets can be a hobby in itself. They might keep up with tech news, watch reviews, or test apps that promise interesting functions.

**Reasons This Appeals**:

**Constant Updates**: Tech evolves quickly, so there is always something new to learn.

**Combining Social and Learning**: They might share their findings on social media or start a small YouTube channel reviewing products.

**Practicality**: Skills learned while tinkering can also help them in their job, making them the go-to person for tech questions.

However, Geminis need to watch their spending if they constantly chase the newest gadget. It might help to set a budget or pace themselves so they are not buying every device that catches their eye.

## Traveling for Fun

When time and budget allow, travel can be a major passion for Geminis. They enjoy seeing new places, trying different foods, and meeting people from varied backgrounds. Traveling meets their thirst for novelty and can create lasting memories—assuming they plan their trips carefully enough to avoid chaos.

**Styles of Travel**:

**Weekend Getaways**: Short trips to nearby towns or parks can suit Geminis who crave a quick change of scenery.

**Longer Vacations**: If they have more time, they might hop between multiple cities or even countries, enjoying the variety.

**Road Trips**: Driving to spots off the main path, stopping whenever something interesting appears, appeals to the Gemini sense of spontaneity.

A potential challenge is staying organized while traveling. If Geminis do not prepare properly, they could forget essential items or end up missing connections. Balancing excitement with planning is key.

## Switching Interests Quickly

One hallmark of Gemini hobbies is that they may dive into an activity with full enthusiasm but lose interest after a short while. For example, they might buy supplies for painting, complete a few pieces, then leave the paints to gather dust because they discovered another pastime.

**Why This Happens**:

**The Thrill of Beginnings**: Starting something new is exciting, and Geminis love that rush of fresh learning.

**Mental Restlessness**: Once they feel they have a basic handle on the hobby, they might long for something different.

**Social Influence**: If their friend group shifts to a new craze, they might follow suit just to keep up with the talk.

It is not necessarily bad to explore many interests, but Geminis could end up feeling scattered or regretting never mastering any one skill. They might also spend more money than intended on gear they barely use.

## Balancing Breadth and Depth

Geminis often ask themselves whether they should keep trying new hobbies or concentrate on a few. Some do not mind being "jacks of all trades," while others eventually want to get deeper into something. Either approach can work, but a bit of balance can help them feel more satisfied.

**Finding That Balance:**

**Pick One Long-Term Hobby**: Choose a pastime that truly sparks joy and try to stick with it for at least several months.

**Leave Room for Small Experiments**: They can still sample other activities, but keep them in short bursts or as occasional treats.

**Reflect on Progress**: If they see improvement in a skill, they might become more motivated to continue.

This way, Geminis get the thrill of new experiences while also building real expertise in at least one area.

## Social Media and Online Communities

For Geminis who enjoy meeting folks with shared interests, online platforms can be a favorite place. They might join gaming communities, chat about favorite shows, or connect on forums about art, cooking, or any hobby imaginable. Exchanging tips and stories with people worldwide can satisfy the Gemini's hunger for conversation.

**Cautions:**

**Time Management**: If they spend too long online, they might not have time to practice the hobbies themselves.

**Distractions**: Social media can lead them down rabbit holes of unrelated content, making it easy to lose focus.

**Over-Involvement**: They might join multiple online groups, which can become overwhelming.

Using online communities wisely can enhance a Gemini's hobbies by learning from others and staying inspired, as long as they do not get buried in endless scrolling.

## Entertaining Friends

Geminis often like to be the host of casual gatherings or game nights. They might plan small parties or dinners where everyone can chat, play games, or share new things they have discovered. This can be a hobby in itself, as Geminis enjoy planning the theme, picking music, or introducing group activities.

**Why This Suits Gemini**:

**Conversation Focus**: They get to chat with multiple people about different topics.

**Creative Options**: They can change up the style of the event each time.

**Bringing People Together**: They often like to see friends mixing and forging new connections.

The main thing to watch is that Geminis do not overcomplicate the plans. Simple, well-managed events can be just as fun as elaborate ones.

## Gaming and Competitions

For Geminis with a competitive side, gaming can be a go-to. Whether it is video games, board games, or puzzle competitions, they often enjoy the mental challenge and the quick thinking required. They might also enjoy the social aspect of multiplayer games, teaming up or facing off against friends.

**Types of Games**:

**Strategy Games**: Geminis can use their ability to see multiple angles to plan moves and anticipate opponents.

**Party Games**: Titles like "Charades" or word games might let them use their wit and keep a lively atmosphere.

**Online Games**: From battle arenas to cooperative quests, Geminis can connect with players around the globe.

They just need to be mindful of how much time they spend gaming if there are other responsibilities waiting. Balance remains important.

## Hobbies with a Purpose

Some Geminis prefer hobbies that also give them a sense of achieving something concrete. This could be home improvement tasks, small business ventures, or community service projects. In each of these, they still get to learn and try fresh ideas, but there is also a result that feels rewarding.

**Possible Outlets**:

**DIY Home Projects**: Painting a room in a new style or fixing up furniture can keep them busy.

**Freelancing**: Offering small creative services online, like graphic design or writing, can blend hobby and earning.

**Volunteering**: Working with a community group can let them meet new people while contributing to a positive cause.

This approach can be especially satisfying if the Gemini sees real-world impact from their efforts, fueling their interest to continue.

## Keeping Motivation in Hobbies

Just like at work, Geminis may face times when they lose the spark for a hobby. The initial excitement fades, or they run into a harder phase of the skill. They might want to shift to something else right away. But sometimes pushing through the dull moments can lead to deeper enjoyment.

**Tactics to Stay Engaged**:

**Break Down Goals**: If they are learning guitar, for instance, set short goals like mastering a single chord progression.

**Join a Club or Group**: Having friends who share the same hobby can keep them motivated to continue.

**Track Improvement**: Looking back to see how far they have come might rekindle enthusiasm.

These steps allow Geminis to see that hobbies can be more than just a fleeting distraction—they can become a source of real growth and joy.

## Balancing Active and Relaxing Pastimes

Geminis often have an active mind, so quiet relaxation might feel unnatural. Yet taking time for calm activities can help them recharge. This might be reading a soothing book, doing light yoga, or simply listening to peaceful music.

**Finding the Right Mix**:

**Schedule Wind-Down Time**: If they spent all day in lively activities, setting aside an hour for a relaxing pastime could prevent burnout.

**Combine Relaxation with Creativity**: For instance, mindful coloring books can let them be creative while also calming the mind.

**Nature Walks**: A slow walk in a park, without any big plan, can help them rest mentally while still satisfying curiosity about their surroundings.

## Involving Friends and Family

Geminis like to share their interests. If they pick up a new hobby, they may invite friends or siblings to try it with them. This can form stronger bonds, as they exchange tips or laugh at mistakes together. However, they should check if others truly want to join, instead of pushing them into something they might not enjoy.

**Examples**:

Teaching a simple dance routine to a friend group.

Hosting a weekend workshop at home for soap-making or candle-making.

Inviting family members to join a group painting session.

Such shared activities can lead to fun memories, and Geminis get to talk about something new—two wins at once.

## Organizing Hobby Time

Because Geminis can gather multiple hobbies, time management might become an issue. They could find themselves flitting from one pastime to another without making real progress in any. If they want to go deeper, it helps to plan how much time each hobby gets.

**Steps for Organizing**:

**Make a Hobby List**: Write down each activity they are currently exploring.

**Rank Them**: Decide which are top priorities and which can be "once in a while" pursuits.

**Set a Weekly Routine**: Perhaps dedicate specific nights or weekends to certain hobbies, so they do not compete for the same time slot.

This method can prevent Geminis from feeling overwhelmed by the sheer number of hobbies they start.

## Collecting as a Hobby

Another pastime some Geminis enjoy is collecting—like stamps, coins, figurines, or comics. Collecting can keep them engaged in searching for new items and learning about the background of each piece. They also get to talk with other collectors and trade details or stories about rare finds.

**Why Geminis Might Like Collecting**:

**Learning Aspect**: Each item might have a story or a unique feature to study.

**Social Connection**: Joining collector groups can lead to lively discussions, trading, and meeting new people.

**Ongoing Variety**: There is always a new item to hunt down, which keeps boredom at bay.

The trick is not letting the collection process get out of control or too expensive. Setting a clear focus can help keep it fun.

## Hobbies for Stress Relief

If Geminis have an active mind prone to anxiety, certain hobbies might help them relax. For instance, gentle yoga, meditation apps, or adult coloring books can slow their thoughts. Even baking can be soothing if they approach it calmly. These pastimes can serve as a balance to the busy side of Gemini life.

**What Works for Stress Relief**:

**Mindful Breathing Exercises**: Short sessions to settle the mind.

**Soothing Crafts**: Activities like knitting or crocheting can be repetitive in a comforting way.

**Light Physical Activities**: Stretching, basic yoga poses, or slow walks can release tension in both body and mind.

Geminis might need to remind themselves to take a step back from fast-paced hobbies once in a while to give their minds a break.

## Traveling Through Media

If a Gemini cannot travel often, they might turn to TV shows, movies, or books that transport them to different worlds or historical periods. This can feed their love of variety without leaving home. They might watch documentaries about places far away or get hooked on fictional adventures that span galaxies.

**Possible Media Picks**:

**Documentaries on Space**: Satisfies curiosity about the universe.

**Shows about Different Cultures**: Helps them learn about people's daily lives in other countries.

**Fantasy Series**: Let them explore imaginative lands full of surprises.

By diving into these stories, Geminis can keep their sense of wonder alive during their downtime.

## Journaling and Reflection

Though Geminis talk a lot, they may not always reflect inwardly about their feelings or growth. Keeping a journal can be a hobby that allows them to analyze the day's events, how they felt, and what they learned. This can also spark new ideas for future projects or topics they want to explore.

**Journaling Benefits**:

**Improved Self-Awareness**: Writing about experiences helps them notice patterns in their behavior and interests.

**Tracking Hobbies**: They can log progress on their current pastime, note any challenges, and plan the next steps.

**Quiet Moment**: Journaling provides a chance to slow down in an otherwise busy mind.

## Combining Hobbies

One way Geminis can keep interest in a hobby longer is by combining it with another interest. For example, if they like writing and also enjoy nature walks, they might create a nature blog. If they love cooking and also love photography, they might photograph their meals to share online.

**Pairing Pastimes**:

**Music + Technology**: Trying digital music creation software.

**Fitness + Social Interaction**: Joining group dance fitness classes that let them chat and exercise together.

**Reading + Discussion**: Forming a small online group to read the same book and meet via video chat to talk about it.

Combining activities can keep the excitement high and let Geminis use their broad interests in a more focused way.

## Letting Go of Old Hobbies

Eventually, a Gemini might find they have too many half-done projects or supplies taking up space. It can be hard to let go, because each reminds them of a fun moment. But clearing out what is no longer used can make room for fresh pursuits.

**Advice for Clearing Out**:

**Evaluate Each Hobby**: Ask, "Am I likely to return to this soon?" If not, maybe it is time to say goodbye.

**Donate or Sell Gear**: Passing it on can give others a chance to enjoy that hobby.

**Keep Fond Memories**: They might take photos of completed items or of them using the gear, so they still have a reminder without clutter.

This process can help Geminis feel lighter and more focused on current activities.

## Staying True to Personal Interests

Sometimes friends or trends push Geminis toward popular hobbies. While it is fine to try them, it is also important to decide which ones truly fit personal tastes. Geminis can ask themselves if they are doing the hobby to please others or because they genuinely like it.

**Tips for Authentic Choices**:

**Notice Joy**: If they are excited to wake up and do the activity, it is likely a good match.

**Check Pressure**: If it feels like a chore or just a way to fit in, it may not be the best pick.

**Combine with Strengths**: Activities that use a Gemini's communication or creative flair can be more satisfying.

By choosing hobbies that resonate with them, Geminis are more likely to stick with them—or at least have a rewarding experience before moving on.

# CHAPTER 13: GEMINI AND HEALTH

When we talk about Gemini and health, it is not just about one single area like physical exercise or mental rest. It is about how people born under this sign might handle their overall well-being—physical, emotional, and everything in between. Geminis are known for being flexible, active thinkers who like to stay occupied. This can affect their health habits in both good and difficult ways. In this chapter, we will look at how Geminis can approach exercise, eating patterns, rest, and self-care. We will also cover common challenges and some ideas for building helpful routines that fit their changeable nature. By understanding these points, Geminis can make choices that support their health in a way that suits their curiosity and lively spirit.

## Linking Mind and Body

Many Geminis move through life with a busy mind, always thinking about ideas or what they can do next. This fast-paced way of living can sometimes lead them to forget about their body's needs. They might skip meals or stay up late because they got wrapped up in a new topic. Over time, these habits can create imbalance. Recognizing that the body needs steady care, just like the mind, is important for Geminis to feel their best.

**Why Mind-Body Balance Matters**:

**Energy Levels**: If Geminis do not get enough rest, their minds might stay active, but their bodies become tired, leading to afternoon slumps or mood dips.

**Reducing Stress**: Tuning into how the body feels can lower the stress that builds up in a racing mind.

**Clear Thinking**: Physical well-being often supports sharper focus and creativity.

## Healthy Eating Patterns

Not every Gemini follows the same eating style, but many can get so focused on chatting, working, or exploring new interests that they either skip meals or grab something quick without thinking about nutrition. Over a long period, this might lead to inconsistent energy levels or issues with digestion.

**Challenges Geminis May Face**:

**Skipping Breakfast**: A Gemini might be in a morning rush, checking messages or thinking of new ideas, and forget to eat a proper breakfast. Later, they feel low on energy or extra hungry.

**Snacking**: Because they are used to switching tasks quickly, Geminis might rely on snacks throughout the day. Some snacks can be healthy (like fruit or nuts), while others might be sugary or salty with limited nutritional value.

**Taste for Variety**: Geminis often enjoy trying different foods. This can be good if they explore nutritious recipes, but it can also lead to sampling a lot of junk food if they are not careful.

**Possible Approaches**:

**Structured Meal Windows**: Even if Geminis dislike strict schedules, having a rough idea—like a morning meal, midday meal, and evening meal—can keep their energy steady.

**Healthy Snack Options**: Storing fruits, nuts, or other nutrient-rich snacks at home or in a bag might help them avoid grabbing junk food.

**Trying New Recipes**: Because Geminis like variety, cooking different healthy dishes can keep them interested in balanced eating. This way, mealtime is not boring.

## Exercise and Movement

Geminis are usually restless in a good way, meaning they like to be on the move. However, not all Geminis engage in regular exercise. Some might sit for hours reading or working on a computer, then feel restless later without knowing why. Finding physical activities that appeal to their quick-thinking nature can help them stay active without getting bored.

**Exercise Ideas for Geminis**:

**Group Classes**: Dance-based fitness or aerobics classes can combine music, social interaction, and fast-paced workouts that keep Geminis interested.

**Sports with Friends**: Joining a casual soccer or basketball game may allow them to chat and have fun while burning off energy.

**Short, Varied Workouts**: If long exercise routines seem dull, a Gemini might break them into quick segments. For example, ten minutes of light cardio in the morning, a short walk at lunchtime, and a fast-paced dance break in the evening.

**Outdoor Adventures**: Hiking or biking in different locations can feed the Gemini love of fresh sights. Each trip feels new, so they stay motivated.

**Sticking with Exercise**:

**Changing It Up**: Every few weeks, a Gemini could pick a slightly different routine or try a new class. This variety can keep them from dropping the habit out of boredom.

**Using Apps or Trackers**: Seeing progress on a fitness app or step counter might encourage them to reach certain goals.

**Workout Buddies**: Doing activities with friends adds a social aspect, making it more fun and harder to skip.

## Rest and Sleep

Because Geminis tend to have busy minds, they might have trouble winding down at night. Some Geminis are "night owls," staying up late to read, chat online, or watch videos. But this habit can lead to less sleep, especially if they still have to wake up early for work or school.

**Common Sleep Challenges**:

**Overthinking Before Bed**: A Gemini might lie awake replaying the day's conversations or planning future activities, making it hard to drift off.

**Irregular Schedule**: One night they stay up until 2 AM, the next they try to sleep at 10 PM, leading to confusion for their body clock.

**Better Sleep Tips**:

**Pre-Bed Routine**: Setting aside 30 minutes before sleep to turn off devices, dim lights, or do something calming (like gentle stretching or reading a relaxing book) can signal the mind to slow down.

**Limit Late-Night Screen Time**: The bright light from phones or tablets can keep the brain awake longer.

**Write Down Thoughts**: Keeping a small notebook by the bed can help Geminis unload ideas or worries. They can write them down to revisit the next day, freeing their mind for rest.

## Managing Stress

Stress can show up quickly for Geminis. Their active minds might jump from worry to worry, or they might take on multiple tasks, feeling excited at first but overwhelmed later. Recognizing the early signs of stress—like irritability, poor sleep, or physical tension—can help them respond in a healthier way.

**Ways to De-Stress**:

**Brief Check-Ins**: Every so often, stop and ask, "How am I feeling right now?" If the answer is tense or uneasy, a short break might help.

**Breathing Exercises**: Taking a few slow, deep breaths can calm both the mind and body.

**Quiet Moments**: Even a Gemini needs stillness sometimes. Activities like coloring, listening to peaceful music, or sitting in a park can refresh their overactive thoughts.

**Talking It Out**: Because Geminis are strong communicators, sharing stress with a friend, family member, or counselor can be healing. They can release their worries through conversation and possibly find useful tips.

## Mental and Emotional Health

People often focus on Gemini's chatty or playful side, but that does not mean Geminis lack deeper emotions. They can carry strong feelings under the surface, sometimes switching between moods more quickly than they would like. Being mindful of their emotional well-being is crucial for a Gemini's overall health.

**Possible Emotional Challenges**:

**Mood Swings**: Jumping from excitement to anxiety or from happiness to low mood in a short span.

**Difficulty Sharing Deep Feelings**: They might be good at talking but still avoid discussing their most personal worries or pains.

**Avoiding Stillness**: Some Geminis dodge tough emotions by staying constantly busy, never giving themselves time to process sadness or frustration.

**Healthy Emotional Habits**:

**Reflective Writing**: Journaling each day, even for five minutes, can help them spot patterns in their moods and feelings.

**Safe Outlets**: Having a trusted friend or professional to confide in can prevent pent-up emotions.

**Relaxation Techniques**: Gentle yoga, guided breathing, or nature walks can offer a calmer space to sort out feelings.

## Doctor Visits and Checkups

Geminis sometimes do not make time for regular checkups or health appointments, especially if they do not feel any big problem. However, routine visits can catch small issues before they become larger and give Geminis the chance to ask health questions they might be curious about.

**Ideas for Keeping Up with Appointments**:

**Mark Calendars**: Set reminders at the start of the year for dental cleanings, physicals, or other checkups so they do not forget.

**Ask Questions**: Geminis typically have many questions. They can use their communication skills to get all the info they need from health professionals.

**Stay Proactive**: If something feels off—like persistent headaches or unusual tiredness—they should not ignore it. Checking sooner can ease worry and address potential issues quickly.

## Building Routine Without Feeling Trapped

A tricky part of health for Geminis can be routine. They like freedom and variety, but many healthy habits—like regular meals, steady sleep, or scheduled exercise—benefit from consistency. So how can a Gemini keep a routine without feeling limited?

**Striking a Balance:**

**Flexible Framework**: They might set basic targets, such as "Exercise three times a week," but keep the activity type flexible so they do not get bored.

**Mini Challenges**: If they want to walk more, they can challenge themselves to reach a certain step count each day, but pick different routes to keep it interesting.

**Mixing Up Meals**: Having a standard meal schedule but rotating recipes or trying different cuisines can keep them curious and on track.

This approach gives them the benefits of routine while still feeding that need for change.

## Finding Motivation

Geminis often do well when they find excitement in what they do, including health-related tasks. If going to the gym feels dull, they may drop it after a few sessions. If a healthy diet feels too restrictive, they might return to random snacks. Therefore, tying health to something motivating is important.

**Examples of Motivating Factors:**

**Social Element**: Working out with a friend or family member can make it fun and create an environment of friendly challenge.

**Apps and Games**: Some fitness apps let users earn points or badges, which can spark a Gemini's playful side.

**Learning Opportunities**: Reading about the science behind nutrition or exercise might engage a Gemini's mind, helping them see how these habits improve the body.

## Seasonal and Environmental Changes

Geminis might also notice that their health patterns shift with changes in season or environment. For instance, they might feel more energetic in the spring when the days lengthen, but sluggish in colder months if they are cooped up indoors.

**Adapting to Seasons**:

**Winter Activities**: Try indoor exercises like a dance video or short workout at home to stay active when it is cold.

**Summer Routines**: If the summer heat is uncomfortable, early-morning or late-evening walks or workouts might fit better.

**Light Therapy**: If short winter days affect mood or energy, using a light box or spending time in brighter areas during midday can help.

## Mindful Eating

We already mentioned how Geminis may skip meals or grab snacks, but there is another layer: mindful eating. This means paying attention to how each bite tastes, how full they feel, and choosing foods that truly satisfy both hunger and health. Because Geminis sometimes speed through tasks, they might also rush meals or eat while checking phones. Slowing down a bit can help digestion and reduce overeating.

**Tips for Mindful Eating**:

**Pause Before Eating**: Take a moment to notice if they are really hungry, or just bored or stressed.

**Chew Slowly**: Put down the fork between bites if needed, focusing on the flavors.

**Limit Distractions**: Eating away from screens can help a Gemini become more aware of portion sizes and fullness cues.

## Handling Energy Ups and Downs

Geminis can go through cycles of high energy followed by periods of tiredness or mental fatigue. One day they may be unstoppable, and the next they might feel like they have no get-up-and-go. Knowing how to handle these swings can support more stable health.

**Balancing Energy**:

**Small Breaks During High-Energy Times**: Taking short rests even when feeling great can prevent burnout the next day.

**Gentle Activity on Low-Energy Days**: Instead of skipping exercise altogether, a light walk or gentle stretch might help maintain momentum.

**Steady Blood Sugar**: Eating balanced meals or healthy snacks on time can avoid sharp energy drops that make a Gemini feel drained.

## Social Circles and Health

Because Geminis often have many friends, these social networks can shape their health habits. If their group mostly meets for fast food late at night, that habit can become normal. On the flip side, if their circle is into sports or group fitness, the Gemini might adopt those positive habits. Being aware of social influences helps Geminis decide if they are forming good or bad routines.

**Making Healthy Social Choices**:

**Suggest Active Meetups**: Instead of just sitting in a café, propose a fun group activity like bowling or a park walk.

**Be Realistic**: If all their friends want pizza, a Gemini can still join but might balance it with a lighter meal earlier or some extra walking that day.

**Encourage Each Other**: Geminis can share their excitement about new healthy recipes or workouts, possibly inspiring friends as well.

## Mental Stimulation as Self-Care

Geminis flourish on mental engagement, which can be a form of self-care. Sometimes, people separate health from intellectual hobbies, but for a

Gemini, activities that stretch the mind can lift mood and reduce stress. Puzzles, reading, or learning new skills can refresh them.

**Why This Matters**:

**Preventing Boredom**: Boredom can lead to unhealthy snacking or negative thoughts. Stimulating activities keep them upbeat.

**Boosting Confidence**: Learning a new skill can make them feel accomplished and happy, which supports emotional health.

**Relaxation in Variety**: If physical rest does not always recharge them, using their mind in a fun, non-work way can serve as an emotional recharge.

Still, it is important to balance mental activities with physical rest, so they are not stuck in constant brain overdrive.

## Setting Realistic Goals

Sometimes, Geminis get excited about a big health goal—like running a marathon or trying a complicated diet plan—and start off with enthusiasm. But if the goal is too large or not broken down into smaller steps, they might drop it mid-way. Setting realistic, shorter targets can help them stay motivated.

**Examples**:

**Walking Before Running**: If they want to become a runner, they can begin with a mix of walking and light jogging, increasing distances gradually.

**Incremental Meal Changes**: Instead of attempting a drastic diet overnight, they can slowly replace less healthy foods with more nutritious options.

**Tracking Small Wins**: Keeping a simple chart of daily or weekly achievements—like the number of days they exercised—can show progress.

Step-by-step achievements often keep Geminis engaged, since each completed step offers a mini sense of excitement or pride.

## Dealing with Information Overload

Geminis love learning, so they might read multiple health articles, watch videos, or listen to various opinions about what is the best diet or exercise. But if the advice is conflicting, a Gemini can become overwhelmed and uncertain about what to do next.

**Ways to Filter Health Information**:

**Seek Trusted Sources**: Check if the information comes from reliable medical or nutritional experts.

**Try One Change at a Time**: If a Gemini wants to test a new approach, doing just one new method and seeing how the body responds can be more helpful than juggling many at once.

**Listen to Their Own Body**: No matter the advice, personal experiences can guide them best. If something causes discomfort or no improvement, it might not be the right fit.

## Creativity in Health Routines

Because Geminis enjoy creativity, adding a sense of fun or novelty to daily health routines can make them more likely to stick around. For instance, they can treat cooking as an experiment, mixing unexpected ingredients. Or they can turn a morning walk into a photo expedition, snapping pictures of interesting sights.

**Fresh Ideas to Keep Routines Interesting**:

**Themed Meals**: Each week, pick a region or style of cuisine to try, focusing on healthy takes on those dishes.

**Music Playlists**: Curate music playlists that align with different workout segments—warm-up, main activity, and cool-down—to keep the experience fresh.

**Healthy Challenges with Friends**: For a month, challenge a friend to see who can drink enough water daily, or who can do a short yoga video each evening. Having fun keeps the routine from feeling like a chore.

## Mindful Breaks During the Day

Geminis often move from one task to another quickly, which can create mental fatigue. Incorporating short, mindful breaks during the day can help them recharge and maintain better mental balance. These breaks do not have to be long—sometimes just a couple of minutes can make a difference.

**Simple Break Activities**:

**Quick Stretch**: Standing up, rolling shoulders, doing a brief forward bend.

**Listening to Calm Music**: Closing eyes and focusing on a favorite tune can reset a busy mind.

**Mini Meditation**: Taking five slow breaths, noticing the inhale and exhale, can bring a sense of calm.

**Stepping Outside**: If possible, a short walk or even stepping onto a balcony to breathe fresh air can refresh thinking.

## Balancing Work and Rest

Many Geminis enjoy being busy. They might fill their schedule with projects, social events, new hobbies, or random outings. While this is fun, it can lead to burnout if they forget to schedule rest or downtime. Balancing active periods with calm intervals is part of good health.

**Signs of Overdoing It**:

**Frequent Headaches or Fatigue**: The body might be signaling that it needs a slower pace.

**Irritability**: Little things at home or work might suddenly feel overwhelming.

**Trouble Focusing**: Despite a normally quick mind, a Gemini might struggle to concentrate if they are overloaded.

## Connection Between Emotions and Physical Health

Geminis can sometimes separate their mental worries from physical symptoms, not realizing they affect each other. Anxiety can lead to upset stomachs or tight muscles. Feeling sad might cause a slump in energy, affecting the desire to exercise. Paying attention to these connections can help them take better care of themselves as a whole.

**Noticing Connections**:

**Body Reaction**: If a Gemini is anxious, do they get headaches or stomachaches? That link can be a warning sign to use stress management tools.

**Physical Tension**: Shoulders or neck feeling sore might signal mental tension, suggesting a need for stretching or relaxation.

**Better Mood After Activity**: If a Gemini sees that a short walk or playing a fun sport lifts their spirits, they can build that into their routine more often.

## Supplements and Vitamins

Some Geminis, eager to improve health, might look into supplements or vitamins. However, with so many products on the market, confusion can arise. While certain vitamins might be helpful, it is best to do research or talk with a professional.

**Tips for Using Supplements**:

**Check With a Professional**: A doctor or nutrition expert can advise which supplements are safe or necessary.

**Avoid Impulse Buys**: Ads might tempt Geminis with promises of quick results. Taking time to investigate can prevent wasting money.

**Stay Organized**: If they do start a vitamin regimen, marking it on a calendar or using a pill organizer can help them remember daily doses.

## Handling Busy Periods in Life

Certain times—like exam seasons, work deadlines, or personal events—can push a Gemini's health habits to the side. In these busy periods, it is easy to default to quick meals, skip workouts, and cut back on sleep. Planning ahead can keep health from crumbling.

**Ways to Cope**:

**Simple Meal Prep**: Cooking a large batch of food at the start of the week can provide easy portions on hectic days.

**Short Exercises**: Even a 10-minute routine is better than none when time is limited.

**Set Sleep Alarms**: Reminding themselves to go to bed at a certain hour can prevent late nights from stacking up.

Once the busy stretch ends, it might take a bit of effort to get back to normal routines, but staying aware helps them bounce back faster.

## Rewarding Small Steps

Geminis tend to be driven by novelty and positive feedback. Recognizing little achievements, like a week of consistent workouts or a few days of balanced meals, can keep them excited about health. While many people think rewards have to be big, even simple acknowledgments can push a Gemini forward.

**Reward Examples**:

**Shared Success**: Telling a friend or posting online, "I kept a healthy breakfast routine all week!" could bring supportive comments.

**Enjoyable Treat**: Buying a new workout T-shirt or piece of music gear might be a small way to applaud themselves without turning to unhealthy sweets.

**Short Relaxation**: Promising themselves an evening with a favorite movie or a calming bath after achieving a week's health goal can also be motivating.

## Self-Compassion When Slipping Up

No one maintains perfect health habits all the time. Geminis can be hard on themselves when they realize they have not exercised in a week or they stayed up late every night. Instead of feeling guilty, it helps to approach slip-ups with understanding and a plan to get back on track.

**Ways to Bounce Back**:

**Identify the Cause**: Did they overbook themselves? Did they lose interest in a routine? Knowing why can help them fix it.

**Plan a Gentle Return**: Start again with small steps—perhaps a 15-minute walk instead of a 45-minute intense workout—to build momentum.

**Positive Self-Talk**: Remind themselves that stumbling is normal, and each day is a chance to begin anew.

# CHAPTER 14: GEMINI AND TECHNOLOGY

Geminis are often labeled as one of the most communicative signs, full of curiosity about the world and eager to connect with many people. Technology naturally supports these traits, offering countless ways to gather facts, keep up with friends, and explore new interests. From phones to social media to advanced gadgets, technology can feel like a wonderland for Geminis—always changing, with something new to learn or try. But technology also has pitfalls, like distractions or privacy concerns, which can be especially tricky for Geminis who are eager to jump into everything. In this chapter, we will look at how Geminis relate to technology, why they might love certain digital tools, and what they can do to maintain a healthier balance in a device-driven age.

## Attraction to Gadgets and Apps

Geminis are usually quick to explore fresh apps or devices, enjoying the excitement of discovering features and possibilities. For example, they might download new social media platforms the moment they appear, or try out a phone with cutting-edge functions. This sense of wonder can keep Geminis up to date in a rapidly evolving tech landscape.

**Reasons This Appeals**:

**Variety**: There are countless apps for communication, gaming, news, productivity, and more, which matches Gemini's love of different experiences.

**Immediate Connections**: With a few taps, Geminis can chat with people around the world, feeding their hunger for conversation.

**Fun of Discovery**: Each new gadget or tool is like a small puzzle to figure out, satisfying their curious mind.

Yet, Geminis might also risk spending too much on the latest devices or juggling so many apps that they get disorganized. Setting a budget or checking if they truly need a new device might help keep impulses in check.

## Social Media Usage

Social media feels tailor-made for the Gemini spirit. They can talk to friends, follow interesting figures, learn random trivia, and see trending topics all in one place. Many Geminis enjoy posting updates about their day or sharing things they find online. They might have multiple accounts across different platforms, each with its own flavor.

**Pros for Geminis**:

**Constant Interaction**: They can receive instant feedback on their thoughts or photos.

**Broad Network**: It is easier to keep in touch with many circles, from close friends to distant acquaintances.

**Exploring Interests**: They can find groups on anything from art to cooking, linking them with others who share niche hobbies.

**Challenges**:

**Distraction**: Frequent notifications can derail a Gemini's focus when they should be working, studying, or resting.

**Emotional Buildup**: Seeing too many posts or arguments might overwhelm them, especially if they feel the need to jump into every conversation.

**Privacy Concerns**: In the rush to share, Geminis might reveal more than intended about their personal life.

## Gathering Information Online

One of the biggest draws of technology for Geminis is the ocean of information at their fingertips. They love to research topics, read about the latest news, and watch videos explaining how things work. If a random question pops into a Gemini's head, they can look up the answer instantly, feeding that never-ending curiosity.

**How This Impacts Them**:

**Rapid Learning**: Geminis can learn a lot on many subjects, expanding their mind quickly.

**Frequent Topic Switching**: They might start reading about space travel, then jump to cooking, then to ancient history, all in one evening.

**Information Overload**: With so much available, a Gemini might feel overwhelmed or spend hours following links, losing track of time.

Balancing curiosity with a sense of direction can help them explore without feeling mentally scattered.

## Using Tech for Organization

Geminis often benefit from digital tools that keep them on track. Since they can lose focus or forget tasks, apps for schedules, to-do lists, or reminders can be a lifesaver. Many Geminis find that setting timers or alarms helps them move from one task to the next. They might also like note-taking apps where they can store quick ideas.

**Recommended Tech for Geminis**:

**Task Management Apps**: Tools like Trello or simple to-do list apps can help them split big projects into smaller goals.

**Calendar Sync**: Digital calendars that sync across phone and computer let them keep track of appointments and events easily.

**Note Apps**: Apps such as Evernote or Google Keep can hold random ideas, web links, or lists Geminis gather throughout the day.

The trick is not to let the planning tools become more interesting than actually finishing tasks. A Gemini might spend too much time customizing their to-do list layout instead of acting on it.

## Tech Habits and Work Life

In the workplace, technology can help Geminis excel. They can use communication tools to collaborate with colleagues, do research, or show presentations. They might also enjoy roles that involve social media management or customer chats, as these keep them in contact with many people.

**Advantages**:

**Speed and Adaptability**: Geminis typically handle new software quickly.

**Online Networking**: They can network with professionals worldwide, sharing ideas and staying ahead of trends.

**Boosting Creativity**: Using design apps or brainstorming tools might help them pitch fresh concepts.

**Pitfalls**:

**Digital Distraction**: While trying to work, a Gemini might sneak onto social media or news sites if they are bored.

**Multi-Tasking Overload**: Juggling multiple chat windows, email threads, and tasks can cause confusion.

Setting guidelines, like using focus modes on their devices, can help them stay productive.

## Gaming and Entertainment

Many Geminis love games—mobile, console, or computer-based. Because games present mental challenges and often have a social aspect (through multiplayer or online communities), Geminis can lose track of time playing them. They might also be drawn to puzzle or trivia apps that let them show off knowledge.

**Positive Sides:**

**Relaxation:** Gaming can be a fun way to unwind.

**Social Interaction:** Playing with friends or joining online groups can satisfy Gemini's chatty nature.

**Strategic Thinking:** Certain games let them exercise quick decision-making, matching their mental agility.

**Caution:**

**Time Sink:** Spending too many hours can cut into rest or other responsibilities.

**Impulsive Spending:** Some games have in-app purchases or microtransactions that can tempt Geminis if they are not careful.

Deciding ahead of time how long to play or setting spending limits can keep gaming from becoming an issue.

## Digital Communication Style

Geminis are known for their communication skills in face-to-face settings, and this often extends to texting, emailing, or messaging online. They might send witty texts, quick jokes, or thoughtful responses. However, misunderstandings can happen if they type too fast or respond impulsively, especially if the topic is serious.

**Good Practices:**

**Reading Before Sending:** Double-checking an important message can prevent typos or abrupt wording.

**Emoji Caution:** While emojis can add fun, sometimes they can be misread if overused or used in serious discussions.

**Timing:** If a Gemini is about to send a big block of text, they might consider if the other person has the time to read it carefully.

Keeping the conversation balanced and respectful can help Geminis maintain strong online relationships.

## Privacy and Digital Boundaries

With their friendly and open nature, Geminis might overshare or forget about digital privacy. They may post personal details on social media or allow many apps to access private data without thinking twice. Later, they could feel uneasy knowing how much of their life is visible.

**Protecting Personal Info**:

**Review App Permissions**: Check which apps have access to location, photos, or contacts. Switch off unneeded permissions.

**Strong Passwords**: Using unique and secure passwords can prevent hacking or identity issues.

**Limit Public Posts**: If they do not want the entire internet to see certain content, adjusting privacy settings or skipping public posts can be wise.

## Tech for Learning and Growth

Geminis thrive on learning, and technology offers countless online courses, tutorials, and lectures. A Gemini might sign up for multiple courses at once, excited to become a mini-expert in different fields. While this is great for mental stimulation, it can also lead to partial course completions if they move on to new interests too soon.

**Advice for Studying Online**:

**Set Clear Goals**: If they are learning a language, pick a target (like finishing a beginner course).

**One Course at a Time**: Focusing on one or two classes keeps them from scattering their efforts.

**Practical Application**: Putting new knowledge into practice (for example, speaking with a native speaker) can maintain interest.

## Balancing Screen Time

A major challenge in modern times is limiting screen time. Geminis could find themselves glued to a phone or computer for hours. Scrolling feeds, watching videos, or chatting can feel exciting, but too much can hurt posture, sleep, and real-world interactions.

**Signs of Excess**:

**Eye Strain**: Frequent headaches, blurry vision, or dry eyes might appear.

**Neglected Tasks**: Household chores or personal goals might get sidelined.

**Lack of Sleep**: Staying up late to watch "one more video" can become a habit.

**Reducing Screen Time**:

**App Time Limits**: Many phones let users set daily app usage caps.

**Device-Free Moments**: Mealtimes or the hour before bed can be screen-free zones.

**Alternate Activities**: If they feel bored, a Gemini might switch to a physical book or a short walk instead of automatically grabbing a device.

## Technology and Relationships

Geminis value communication, so they may use messaging apps and video calls to keep close ties with loved ones. This can be wonderful for bridging distance. However, too much digital contact might reduce face-to-face interactions, or cause them to rely on quick text chats when a deeper conversation is needed.

**Finding Balance**:

**Quality Over Quantity**: Instead of multiple shallow messages, aim for a thoughtful call or an in-person meetup if possible.

**Shared Tech Activities**: Watching a show together online, playing co-op games, or working on a digital project can be a fun joint experience.

**Offline Bonding**: Even if they text often, planning real-world get-togethers can keep relationships strong.

## Tech Work vs. Tech Recreation

Some Geminis merge tech into their work, maybe in digital marketing, content creation, or coding. Others primarily see tech as fun. Either way, they might risk burnout if they spend their workday on a computer, then spend free hours gaming or scrolling social media. The brain may never get a break from screens.

**Strategy to Separate**:

**Physical Hobbies**: Trying sports, crafts, or cooking after work can give the mind a screen-free rest.

**Clear End of Work**: Logging off email and work apps at a certain time helps them switch from "work mode" to personal time.

**Tech Sabbaticals**: Now and then, taking a day or weekend with minimal device use can refresh their mental energy.

## Online Friendships and Communities

Geminis often enjoy being part of online groups—forums, fan clubs, or social media circles—because it gives them access to people from different walks of life. They might discuss favorite shows, share memes, or debate new ideas. While these friendships can be real and meaningful, they should also be mindful of potential drama or negativity in big communities.

**Tips for Healthy Online Interactions**:

**Pick Positive Spaces**: Not all corners of the internet are friendly. Finding groups with respectful rules can limit fights or toxic behavior.

**Limit Heated Debates**: Geminis love discussions, but too many arguments can be draining. Knowing when to step away helps.

**Protect Personal Data**: Not everyone online is who they say they are, so being cautious with personal info is wise.

## Digital Creativity

Geminis may feel drawn to expressing themselves online. They could start a blog, record podcasts, or create videos to share opinions or teach something they have learned. This can be a wonderful way to let their voice shine, as long as they keep consistency and do not abandon projects too quickly.

**Ways to Express**:

**Podcasting**: Chatting about favorite topics or interviewing interesting people can harness their strong communication.

**YouTube or Streaming**: Showing gaming sessions, makeup tutorials, or cooking demos can let them interact live with viewers.

**Art Portfolios**: Posting drawings, photos, or digital art can attract like-minded fans and peers.

It is important to manage expectations, though. Growing an audience often takes time, and a Gemini might lose patience if they do not see quick feedback. Keeping the focus on enjoyment can help them stick with it longer.

## Evolving Tech Interests

As technology changes, Geminis might always be looking for the newest social trend, phone feature, or online community. They might try VR headsets, experiment with AI tools, or jump into new content platforms. This constant shift can be exciting but can also scatter their attention.

**Suggestions**:

**Set Purposeful Goals**: Ask, "What do I want to gain from this new tech?" If it is purely curiosity, that is fine, but having a specific aim can prevent time-wasting.

**Create Time Blocks**: If they want to test a new gadget or platform, scheduling a certain window for it avoids letting the entire day slip away.

**Revisit Old Favorites**: Before dropping a previous tool or platform, consider if there is still value in using it. Sometimes, stable tools can be more beneficial than chasing every new release.

## Online Learning vs. In-Person Learning

Geminis love learning in general. With technology, they can access digital classrooms, watch video lectures, or join online workshops. Yet, some Geminis also gain a lot from face-to-face discussions. Balancing both might enrich their experience.

**Choosing the Right Format**:

**Online Courses**: Flexible scheduling, broad topics, good for self-driven learners.

**In-Person Classes**: Offers direct interaction, immediate Q&A, and personal connections, which a Gemini may value.

**Hybrid Mix**: Some classes combine online resources with occasional in-person meets, giving Geminis the best of both worlds.

## Managing Notifications

With multiple apps and channels, Geminis may get constant pings—messages, updates, event reminders, or social media tags. Each alert can break concentration, leading to a fragmented work or study session. Learning to tame notifications can reduce stress and help them focus.

**Notification Control**:

**Custom Settings**: Turn off unimportant notifications, keep only vital ones.

**Silent Periods**: Use "Do Not Disturb" mode during key work or rest times.

**Group Check-Ins**: Instead of checking each notification immediately, pick specific times to review messages or posts in a batch.

## Healthy Online-Offline Balance

Geminis might feel anxious if they are offline, worried they could miss news or interesting conversations. But constant connectivity can also raise anxiety. Finding a healthy balance means acknowledging that not every update is critical.

**Practical Steps**:

**Digital-Free Zones**: Keeping devices out of the bedroom at night can improve sleep quality.

**Set Offline Goals**: Plan daily tasks or hobbies that require no screen, like cooking a new dish or reading a printed book.

**Real-Time Experiences**: Encourage face-to-face meetups with friends, nature walks, or art sessions as part of the weekly routine.

## Tech and Family Life

For Geminis with family responsibilities, technology can be both helpful and distracting. They might use parenting apps or schedule tools, but also get lost in social media when they should spend time with kids or partners. Striking a balance is essential for healthy family relationships.

**Tips for Family Tech Use**:

**Shared Guidelines**: If kids are old enough, set rules about device usage for everyone, including parents.

**Group Activities**: Watching a movie together or playing a family-friendly game can be a bonding experience, rather than each person isolated on a personal screen.

**Tech-Free Gatherings**: During meals or special events at home, consider a no-phone rule to focus on real interaction.

## Online Security and Scams

Because Geminis are open and curious, they could fall for tricky links, suspicious downloads, or scam messages if they act quickly without careful thought. Learning basic online security can protect them from identity theft or other trouble.

**Essential Security Habits**:

**Question Strange Links**: If an offer or message looks too good to be true, it probably is.

**Update Software**: Regularly updating apps and operating systems fixes vulnerabilities.

**Use Two-Factor Authentication**: Adding an extra layer of login protection can keep accounts safer.

## Tech as a Career Path

Some Geminis might choose careers in fields like programming, digital marketing, content creation, or data analysis. Their adaptability and communication strengths can serve them well, but they also need to watch for boredom if a role becomes too repetitive. Seeking positions that let them innovate or interact with many people can be ideal.

**Potential Tech Careers**:

**Social Media Manager**: Perfect for Geminis who enjoy online conversations and keeping up with trends.

**User Experience (UX) Researcher**: Involves understanding how people use products, matching Gemini's interest in different viewpoints.

**Tech Support or Help Desk**: They can talk to diverse clients, use problem-solving skills, and learn about various tech issues.

## Innovation and Experimentation

Given their quick minds, Geminis might explore building their own apps or websites, even if just as a hobby. They might experiment with coding tutorials or design programs to see if they can craft something useful or entertaining. This can be rewarding, but they should be prepared for a steep learning curve if they are new to it.

**Staying Motivated**:

**Focus on Small Projects**: Rather than starting a huge app, begin with simpler tasks and scale up.

**Collaborate with Others**: Sharing projects with friends or online communities can keep them engaged and gather helpful feedback.

## Tech Anxiety and FOMO

"FOMO" (fear of missing out) can be strong for Geminis, who love being in the know. They might check their phone constantly to see if something exciting happened online. However, this can lead to anxiety or a feeling that they can never fully unplug.

**Coping with FOMO**:

**Regular Offline Breaks**: Remind themselves that real life continues outside digital spaces. Missing a meme or conversation does not ruin their life.

**Practice Gratitude**: Focusing on what they have in the present moment can reduce the urge to chase every new update.

**Limit Social Comparisons**: Realizing that online profiles often show only highlights can help them avoid feeling they are missing out on bigger experiences.

## Taking Digital Detoxes

Now and then, a digital detox—switching off from devices for a set time—can do wonders for a Gemini's mental clarity. They might feel restless at first, but a day or weekend away from constant notifications can refresh their mind, giving them a calmer perspective when they return.

**Successful Detox Steps**:

**Warn Contacts**: Let friends or coworkers know they will be offline, so they do not worry about a sudden lack of response.

**Plan Fun Offline Activities**: Reading physical books, painting, cooking, or spending time outdoors can fill that gap.

**Reflect on Feelings**: After the detox, note if they felt less anxious, more relaxed, or had better concentration.

# CHAPTER 15: GEMINI AND THEIR ENVIRONMENT

Geminis have many interests and can shift their focus quickly. This same style often shows up in how they relate to their surroundings—whether that is their living space, neighborhood, or the natural environment around them. If you watch a Gemini in different settings, you might notice that they respond to new places with excitement, or they rearrange their rooms on a whim. Understanding this connection to their environment can help Geminis build surroundings that keep them active, comfortable, and able to explore ideas freely.

In this chapter, we will look at how Geminis interact with the spaces around them and why variety plays such a big part in their comfort. We will also see how Geminis can create harmony in different environments—indoors and outdoors—while avoiding boredom. By paying attention to these points, a Gemini can feel grounded in their environment, even as they keep their minds open to fresh experiences.

## Craving Variety in Their Surroundings

A key trait of Gemini is the desire for newness and change. This can affect how they set up their homes or offices. A Gemini might dislike monotony or having everything in the same place for too long. The environment often needs to spark their curiosity, give them room for mental stimulation, or simply avoid feeling "stuck."

**Rearranging Rooms**: Some Geminis enjoy moving furniture around every so often. It gives them a sense of novelty. One day, the couch might face a window; a week later, they might shift it to face the TV.

**Changing Décor**: They might experiment with different color themes or small decorative pieces, switching them out according to their mood or a new interest.

**Trying Different Spots to Work or Relax**: Instead of always sitting at the same desk, a Gemini may rotate between a reading nook, a kitchen table, or even the floor with cushions. This variety keeps them energized.

This craving for variety can be very personal. One Gemini might move items every week, while another might do it once every few months. The main idea is that a Gemini typically feels better if they know they can shift things around when they want.

## Needing Both Social and Private Spaces

Geminis often have a social side, enjoying conversations and group activities. They also have times when they want a quiet spot to concentrate on a topic or read in peace. Balancing these two needs in their environment can keep them from feeling restless or overwhelmed.

**A Space to Host Friends**: Many Geminis like having an area in their home—maybe a living room or a cozy corner—where they can invite friends to chat, play games, or discuss new ideas. This might include comfortable seating in a circle, so everyone can see each other and talk easily.

**A Personal Corner**: At the same time, Geminis often benefit from a personal retreat, like a small office, a reading chair by a window, or a desk with a lamp. Here, they can read, journal, or brainstorm without interruption.

**Being Strategic in Small Homes**: If a Gemini lives in a smaller space, they might set up multifunctional areas. For example, a corner of the bedroom could double as a reading spot during quiet time but transform into a social hangout spot with floor cushions when guests come over.

Learning to create both group-friendly and solo-friendly areas helps Geminis avoid feeling like they lack either social engagement or personal reflection time.

## Airy, Bright Environments

Gemini is an air sign, and many people born under this sign feel at ease in airy, bright spaces. That can mean open windows, natural light, and proper ventilation. Stuffy, cramped rooms may leave them feeling sluggish or blocked in their thinking.

**Why Light and Air Matter:**

**Boosting Mood**: Sunlight can lift spirits and reduce the dullness that closed-off spaces create.

**Encouraging Movement**: When air flows, Geminis might feel more relaxed strolling around the house, stretching, or sitting in different areas.

**Fostering Mental Clarity**: Many Geminis find they think better in bright or breezy rooms, which can help them come up with new ideas.

**Ways to Achieve This:**

**Opening Windows**: Letting fresh air in, even for part of the day, can make the environment feel more alive.

**Sheer Curtains**: If possible, using lighter curtains can let sunlight enter while still offering some privacy.
**Plenty of Plants**: Indoor plants can filter the air and create a fresh feel. They also add a bit of natural variety, which resonates with Gemini's curiosity.

## City Life vs. Rural Settings

Not every Gemini lives in a bustling city, but many do enjoy urban settings because they offer stimulation, events, and a chance to discover new places. On the other hand, some Geminis find the quiet of a rural environment soothing—especially if they can still socialize or keep varied activities going.

**Urban Attraction:**

**Endless Options**: A city might have many cafes, libraries, and community events. Geminis can check out different spots, meeting new people or trying new foods.

**Energy Flow**: Crowded sidewalks, bright lights, and the rush of people can make Geminis feel they are in the center of action, which can be exciting.

**Public Transportation**: Buses or trains can let them move around without being tied to one place, which suits their flexible style.

**Rural or Suburban Appeal**:

**Mental Rest**: Some Geminis, while loving variety, might appreciate open green spaces or quiet streets. It gives them a chance to think or work on creative ideas.

**Close-Knit Community**: Smaller towns can offer friendly neighbors or local gatherings that let Geminis connect more personally, though the variety might be less than a city.

**Nature Access**: If there are trails, lakes, or gardens nearby, Geminis can go explore whenever they need a break.

Geminis can be happy in either setting, as long as they find ways to satisfy their curiosity and social needs. For city-based Geminis, it might mean balancing the noise with a calm corner at home. For rural-based Geminis, it could involve occasionally traveling to urban areas or setting up social clubs to keep things lively.

## Adaptability in Different Climates

Geminis are known for adaptability, but that does not mean they like extreme temperatures or never struggle with climate changes. In fact, they can be sensitive to drastic changes—like scorching heat or icy winters—if these conditions block them from going out to explore. Still, their flexible attitude often helps them find ways to manage.

**Handling Heat**: Geminis might keep fans or air-conditioning on in the summer, or plan outings early in the morning or late in the evening when it is cooler. They could also switch up their wardrobe, favoring light fabrics that feel airy.

**Handling Cold**: In chilly seasons, they might layer clothing, keep warm blankets or cozy rugs around the house, and drink hot beverages while reading or chatting with friends online.

**Switching Activities**: If the weather outside is not comfortable, Geminis can redirect their curiosity indoors—maybe exploring online museums, trying new indoor hobbies, or rearranging their living space.

This flexibility allows them to remain engaged with life, regardless of whether the sun is blazing or the snow is falling.

## Personal Organization vs. Clutter

Some Geminis work best in a slightly chaotic environment, with papers, notes, or books everywhere. Others prefer a neat, minimalist space that avoids distractions. In reality, many Geminis fall in between: they want a place where they can see the items that spark ideas but do not want a total mess that slows them down.

**Finding the Right Balance**:

**Open Storage**: Shelves where books and objects are visible might be appealing. This way, a Gemini can glance around and pick what they want to read or use next.

**Clutter Zones**: If a Gemini needs to spread out certain projects or materials, they might designate one table or corner for "work in progress," while keeping the rest of the space tidier.

**Regular Sorting**: Now and then, going through old papers or items and discarding what is no longer needed helps them stay organized. This process can feel like a mini adventure—Geminis might rediscover old ideas or notes that spark new creativity.

A healthy environment for a Gemini often includes some openness to keep ideas flowing, but not so much clutter that they feel overwhelmed or cannot find what they need.

## Bringing Nature Indoors

Since Geminis like variety, they may enjoy having elements of nature inside their living spaces. This can mean plants, small water fountains, or natural textures. It adds another layer of stimulation and may help them feel connected to the wider world, even if they are in a city apartment.

**Plant Life**: Succulents, herbs, or easy-to-care-for houseplants can bring color and fresh air. Watching a plant grow offers daily interest for someone who likes small changes.

**Natural Materials**: Furniture or decor made from wood, stone, or bamboo might give a Gemini's environment a calm yet diverse feel.

**Light and Scents**: They might experiment with essential oils or scented candles that remind them of forests, oceans, or gardens. These small details can help keep the senses engaged.

## Gemini's Approach to Environmental Issues

Beyond personal space, some Geminis show a strong interest in broader environmental topics. They might read articles about sustainability, climate, or conservation and want to join discussions or activities that address these issues. Their ability to gather facts quickly can make them persuasive in sharing information.

**Possible Environmental Efforts**:

**Recycling and Reusing**: A Gemini might set up a simple recycling system at home or choose reusable items to reduce waste.

**Community Projects**: Some Geminis like volunteering in clean-up drives or supporting local green initiatives—partly for the social aspect and partly for the cause.

**Spreading the Word**: With strong communication skills, Geminis might post tips on social media or talk with friends about ways to protect the environment. They can become advocates, encouraging people to adopt small planet-friendly steps.

While not every Gemini is deeply involved in environmental activism, those who are might find it rewarding to blend their love of ideas with real-world impacts.

## Seasonal Décor and Themes

Because Geminis enjoy switching things up, they may also like adjusting their environment with each season. This could mean redecorating or adding small touches that match the mood of the time of year. It gives them fresh stimulation without a big overhaul.

**Ideas**:

**Spring Touches**: Light colors, fresh flowers, or prints that remind them of new growth.

**Summer Vibes**: Bright pillows, beach-inspired elements, or fun wall art that feels light and cheerful.

**Autumn Atmosphere**: Warm colors, small pumpkins, or leaf designs around the home to mirror the fall outside.

**Winter Comfort**: Soft blankets, fairy lights, or cozy rugs to create a snug indoor environment.

Even small changes—a new tablecloth, a wreath, or some seasonal art—can keep a Gemini's environment feeling lively and fresh.

## Travel and Temporary Environments

Geminis love to move around, often traveling for fun or visiting new places. They can adapt quickly to unfamiliar hotel rooms, friend's couches, or shared lodging. This flexibility means they usually do not mind changing their environment for short periods, as long as it offers something new or interesting.

**Tips for Feeling at Home While Traveling**:

**Carry Comfort Items**: A Gemini might pack a favorite blanket, pillow, or small memento to personalize any space.

**Explore the Local Scene**: Once they arrive, they can walk the neighborhood, find a café, or visit a local market to feel connected to the place.

**Stay Open-Minded**: If the accommodations are simpler or less comfortable than expected, Geminis can focus on the adventure aspect of trying something different.

Every trip can become a chance for Geminis to gather new impressions, stories, and experiences, all of which they bring back to their usual environment later.

## Maintaining a Workspace

Whether at home or in an office, Geminis need a workspace that allows them to focus but also tap into their creativity. While the perfect setup varies, certain elements can help them stay productive without losing interest:

**Essential Elements**:

**Desk Layout**: If possible, a Gemini might want a spacious desk so they can keep notes, a laptop, or reference materials in sight.

**Visual Inspiration**: A pinboard or wall art that shows interesting quotes, images, or color swatches can stir new ideas.

**Changeable Stations**: Sometimes, a Gemini might shift from desk to a standing area, or even a beanbag, to avoid feeling glued to one spot.

A flexible workspace is vital for Geminis, helping them manage tasks and brainstorming sessions in ways that match their mental flow.

## Social Events in the Gemini Environment

Inviting people over can be a highlight for Geminis who enjoy playing host. They might set up events—like a board game night, a book discussion, or an informal get-together—where everyone can talk, share opinions, or learn something new.

**Hosting Tips:**

**Multiple Conversation Zones**: Placing chairs or cushions in small groups around the room can let guests form different clusters of talk, which Geminis can float between.

**Light Snacks**: Having finger foods or simple meals can keep energy going. Geminis may even try unique or unexpected recipes, adding another talking point.

**Interactive Activities**: Instead of one big activity, they could offer varied stations—maybe a puzzle on one table, a music playlist in another corner—so guests can sample what interests them.

These gatherings often reflect Gemini's environment: flexible, welcoming, and buzzing with ideas.

## Balancing Calm and Stimulation

Because Geminis thrive on stimulation, they might fill their environment with bright colors, fun objects, or constant background music. However, too much stimulation can lead to restless energy. Balancing busy spots with calmer corners can help them avoid overload.

**Small Ways to Add Calm:**

**Soft Lighting**: Having lamps with adjustable brightness can set a calm tone when needed.

**Quiet Hours**: A Gemini could designate part of the day—or the late evening—for quiet activities, with devices turned off or on silent.

**Minimalist Corners**: Even if the living room is vibrant, a corner in the bedroom could be kept simple—a few essential items—to let the mind rest.

This balance ensures that the environment is neither overly stimulating nor too dull for a Gemini's liking.

## Personalizing Without Overspending

Geminis may be tempted to buy new décor items often. Yet constantly purchasing things can strain budgets and lead to clutter. They can still personalize their surroundings in cost-effective ways:

**DIY Upgrades**: Painting an old shelf in a bright color, making artwork from photos, or crafting unique decorations can keep costs down and spark creativity.

**Swapping with Friends**: Trading décor or furnishings with friends can freshen up the look without spending money.

**Rotating Items**: Keeping some items stored and then bringing them out while storing others helps the home look different without requiring new purchases.

## Soundscapes and Music Choices

For many Geminis, background sound can shape their mood. Some like instrumental music while they work, while others enjoy nature sounds or silence. Adjusting these audio elements can help them stay focused or relaxed.

**Music for Work**: Geminis might pick playlists that are energetic yet not too distracting. They could try different genres: classical, lo-fi beats, or soft rock, depending on the task at hand.

**Music for Relaxation**: Ambient sounds of rain, gentle piano, or nature recordings can help quiet the mind.

**Sound Control**: If living in a noisy neighborhood, noise-canceling headphones or thick curtains might be needed. For Geminis who want a livelier atmosphere, leaving a window open to city sounds could feel inspiring.

## Gemini at School or Shared Housing

Many Geminis spend time in shared environments, like dorm rooms or shared apartments. Co-living can be both exciting and challenging. A Gemini might love meeting new roommates but might struggle if there is too much or too little variety in how the shared space is used.

**Co-living Tips**:

**Mutual Agreement**: Talking early about cleaning schedules or noise levels can prevent conflicts.

**Personal Touches**: Even if they only have a small corner, adding personal décor or a tiny desk can let a Gemini express themselves.

**Respect Others**: While Geminis might enjoy changing the common area's look, they should consider if roommates like changes or prefer stability.

## Gemini's Connection to Outdoor Environments

Beyond indoor spaces, Geminis can find energy in outdoor settings like parks, beaches, or trails. They often see these locations as blank pages where they can walk, think, or chat with friends.

**Outdoor Activities**:

**Picnics and Gatherings**: A Gemini might invite people for a casual meet-up at the park, bringing games or musical instruments.

**Solo Walks**: Strolling in nature can clear the mind and spark new ideas.

**Community Gardens**: If available, they might help out in a local garden to learn about plants and meet neighbors.

Outdoor spaces can break the routine of indoor life and feed a Gemini's curiosity about the world.

## Digital and Physical Worlds Combined

As seen in earlier chapters, Geminis often like technology. They might use apps to explore local spots, track how they organize rooms, or share photos of their environment online. This blend of digital and physical space can be fun, but it should be managed so that they do not lose touch with the real, tangible surroundings.

**Examples of Blended Approaches**:

**Mood Boards**: Using a digital pinboard to gather décor ideas or color schemes, then experimenting in real life.

**Location Apps**: Checking online listings of new cafés or events, then going out to see them in person.

**Smart Home Devices**: A Gemini might enjoy voice-activated lights or music systems that respond to their ever-shifting mood.

## Handling Sudden Changes in the Environment

Life can toss unexpected shifts: a move to a new place, a roommate leaving, or changes in the neighborhood. Geminis generally do well with shifts if they see them as chances for fresh experiences. But large changes can still feel stressful if they are forced, not chosen.

**Coping Strategies**:

**Focus on Possibilities**: Thinking, "What new benefits could this change bring?" can keep a Gemini's mindset upbeat.

**Carrying Over Familiar Comforts**: Even if they move to another city, bringing treasured décor, books, or habits can give continuity.

**Stay Flexible**: Recognizing that the environment might evolve further helps them remain open to future adaptations.

## Incorporating Learning Zones

Geminis love learning. In their home or environment, setting up small learning zones can spark that craving for knowledge. It might be a corner with a globe and travel books, a place to practice an instrument, or a table for science experiments.

**Benefits of a Learning Zone:**

**Encourages Exploration**: Having materials in plain sight can prompt a Gemini to pick up a book or try a puzzle spontaneously.

**Shows Progress**: Visible reminders—like a language chart on the wall—let them track their improvement.

**Makes Study Fun**: Decorating the zone with colorful notes or posters can turn studying into an enjoyable part of daily life, rather than a chore.

## Environmental Routine vs. Spontaneity

While Geminis like variety, they might benefit from a little routine in how they treat their environment. For instance, having a scheduled cleaning day or a set time to open windows for fresh air. Yet they can still keep spontaneity in other areas—like spontaneously deciding to move a piece of furniture or changing up the décor.

**Combining Both:**

**Routine Tasks**: Keep them short and consistent, so they do not feel burdensome.

**Flexible Décor Choices**: Decide on small monthly changes—a new poster or switching a lamp's location—so they have something to look forward to.

**Allow Spontaneous Moments**: If they suddenly feel like putting fairy lights on a bookshelf, they can go for it without second-guessing. This sense of freedom balances with the helpful structure of a baseline routine.

## Handling Clashes with Others About Space

If a Gemini shares a home with people who prefer everything to stay the same—like a partner, family member, or roommate—they might disagree over rearranging furniture or adding bright colors. Learning to discuss changes calmly is key.

**Tips for Peaceful Resolutions**:

**Explain Reasons**: Geminis can share why a change is exciting or helpful, rather than just doing it and surprising everyone.

**Find Compromises**: Maybe they can switch up their personal area while leaving common areas as they are, or make small changes that do not disrupt others.

**Plan Joint Projects**: Working together to choose a new color or item can turn it into a shared activity.

## Environmental Harmony for Health

We discussed health in a previous chapter, but environment plays a big role here too. A clean, airy, and uplifting space can aid both physical well-being and mental relaxation. For Geminis, designing a space with room to move, good air quality, and spots for quiet rest can lessen stress.

**Small Enhancements**:

**Scent**: Using mild scents like lavender or citrus can energize or calm a Gemini at different times of day.

**Lighting**: If possible, use natural light in the morning to wake up gently, and softer lights in the evening to wind down.

**Organization for Calm**: Knowing where important items are (like keys or favorite books) can reduce frantic searching, which can stress a Gemini on busy days.

# CHAPTER 16: COMMON MYTHS ABOUT GEMINI

Geminis can be one of the most talked-about zodiac signs, with countless jokes, memes, and comments floating around about who they are and how they act. While each sign has its own set of stereotypes, Gemini often finds itself at the center of certain labels that may not always reflect reality. Sometimes these myths arise from an exaggerated view of the "twins" symbol, or from misunderstanding the Gemini love for variety.

In this chapter, we will break down some of the most common myths tied to Gemini personalities. By examining them carefully, we can see where they come from and why they are oversimplified. We will also highlight the truths that may lie underneath or the ways Geminis can respond to these myths. Remember, while a person's zodiac sign can offer clues about general tendencies, everyone is unique, shaped by personal experiences, background, and choices.

## Myth: "Geminis Have Two Faces and Cannot Be Trusted"

One of the biggest myths about Gemini is that they are "two-faced" or insincere. People often interpret the twins symbol as meaning that Geminis will say one thing but secretly think another, or that they cannot be honest in their relationships. This stereotype is one of the harshest and most widely spread.

**Why This Myth Exists**:

**Twins Symbol**: The sign of the twins sometimes leads people to assume it represents two clashing personalities, even though the symbol can also stand for flexibility or seeing different angles.

**Quick Changes**: Geminis can change opinions if they learn new information or see a different angle, which some might mistake for dishonesty.

**Adaptable Speech**: Because Geminis often talk to many kinds of people, they might adjust how they communicate, leading others to think they are being fake.

**The Reality**:

**Open-Mindedness**: Changing viewpoints does not always mean deceit; it can also mean Geminis are open-minded.

**Social Adaptation**: If Geminis alter their tone in different social circles, it is usually about kindness and fitting the context, not tricking anyone.

**Varied Interests**: A Gemini may show excitement about many topics, which might look like a split personality to outsiders, but it is often sincere enthusiasm for multiple viewpoints.

## Myth: "Geminis Never Stop Talking"

Geminis have a reputation for chatting, which can lead to the myth that they are always talking and never listening. People might joke that once a Gemini starts, you cannot get a word in. While Geminis are known for communication, this does not mean they are incapable of being good listeners or staying quiet when needed.

**Why This Myth Exists**:

**Mercury Influence**: Astrology links Gemini with Mercury, the planet associated with speech and thought, which suggests a strong inclination to communicate.

**Lively Personalities**: Some Geminis do love sharing ideas or telling stories, giving the impression they are constantly in talk mode.

**The Reality**:

**Talking as Connection**: Geminis often talk to connect with others, gather knowledge, or share interesting facts. They do not do it just to hear themselves speak.

**Moments of Silence**: Many Geminis also have times when they reflect quietly, read, or study without speaking. They might not always show this side in large groups, but it is there.

**Aware of Setting**: In formal or serious situations, Geminis can modulate how much they speak. They are not oblivious to context, even if they lean toward openness.

## Myth: "Geminis Are Flaky and Always Cancel Plans"

Some people believe that Geminis cannot be counted on because they get bored or change their mind. They might say Geminis set up events but then back out at the last moment, leaving friends disappointed. While it is true that Geminis enjoy spontaneity, labeling them all as unreliable is too broad.

**Why This Myth Exists**:

**Love of Variety**: Geminis may switch plans if they see something they think is more interesting. This can be misunderstood as flakiness.

**Overcommitment**: Sometimes they say yes to too many invitations because it all sounds fun at first, and then they realize they cannot fulfill them all.

**Curious Nature**: Their curiosity leads them to check out multiple events or tasks, which can strain their schedule.

**The Reality**:

**Effort to Improve**: Many Geminis learn to manage their time better, using reminders or calendars to avoid double-booking.

**Balance**: If they care about certain plans, they will stick to them. The key is finding the events or friendships that matter the most to them.

**Flexibility**: In some cases, what looks like flakiness might be a result of genuine scheduling mishaps rather than a lack of caring.

## Myth: "Geminis Are Emotionally Shallow"

Because Geminis are viewed as logical or talkative, some people think they do not feel things deeply. They might assume that Geminis prefer to stay on the surface of topics or quickly move on if emotions get too intense. However, this overlooks the fact that Geminis can experience strong feelings; they just may show them differently.

**Why This Myth Exists:**

**Conversation Focus:** Geminis often talk about ideas or outside interests rather than personal feelings in group settings, which can look like avoiding depth.

**Adaptability:** Switching moods or interests might lead others to believe they do not take anything seriously.

**Rational Approach:** Some Geminis try to solve emotional issues with logic, which can seem detached.

**The Reality:**

**Private Emotions:** Many Geminis do process emotions, but they might need alone time or a one-on-one talk rather than a public display.

**Dual Expression:** A Gemini can be both logical and emotional, using reason to handle feelings without ignoring them.

**Varied Reactions:** Not all Geminis are the same. Some openly show emotions, while others keep them guarded until they trust someone.

## Myth: "Geminis Cannot Focus on Anything for Long"

Another stereotype is that Geminis lack focus and will drop a project as soon as it is no longer interesting. While some Geminis do enjoy starting new tasks, they can—and often do—complete things that truly capture their passion.

**Why This Myth Exists:**

**Short Attention Span:** Geminis do like variety, and they might jump between interests.

**Multiple Projects:** Seeing them juggle many ideas at once can leave the impression they do not finish any.

**Excitement-Based:** Once the excitement fades, a Gemini might indeed move on unless they find fresh ways to stay engaged.

**The Reality:**

**Finishing When It Matters:** When Geminis truly care about a goal, they find strategies—like breaking tasks into steps—to stay motivated.

**Task Rotation:** Having several parallel projects does not necessarily mean none will be finished. Geminis may complete them in a rotation style.

**Adapted Focus:** Many Geminis develop time-management skills and learn to keep their curiosity satisfied while still reaching outcomes.

## Myth: "Geminis Are Always Party People"

Geminis might love social gatherings and chatting with new people. However, painting all Geminis as nonstop partygoers is a stretch. Many Geminis enjoy quiet nights of reading or doing creative work just as much as a fun hangout.

**Why This Myth Exists:**

**Social Approach:** Gemini is known for good conversation, so it is assumed they are party-focused.

**Public Image:** Observers see Geminis being lively in groups and think that is how they spend all their time.

**The Reality:**

**Introverted Geminis:** Some prefer smaller groups or one-on-one talks, finding big crowds draining.

**Balancing Social and Solo:** Even outgoing Geminis need downtime to reflect, plan, or rest. They might love a party but also enjoy a quiet Sunday with a book or puzzle.

**Choice of Party:** A Gemini might attend events that offer something new—like a theme or an unusual location—rather than going to random parties just for the sake of it.

## Myth: "Geminis Are Deceitful Flirts"

Another myth suggests that Geminis flirt with everyone and cannot stick to a single partner. Critics say they enjoy playing games with people's affections. While some Geminis can be playful in conversation, labeling them as automatically unfaithful or manipulative is unfair.

**Why This Myth Exists:**

**Lighthearted Talk:** If Geminis joke or banter in a friendly way, others might mistake that for flirting.

**Excitement for New People:** They do enjoy meeting fresh faces, which can be seen as flirtatious.

**Inconsistent Communications:** If a Gemini's mood shifts, it might confuse someone into thinking they are playing with emotions.

**The Reality:**

**Friendly Nature:** Many Geminis are just social and like hearing about people's experiences, which can come across as flirtation.

**Choice to Commit:** A Gemini who truly cares about a person can be loyal. The key is that they want mental stimulation and honest communication from the relationship.

**Directness**: If they feel a strong bond, Geminis often express it openly. They might handle breakups or changes in a straightforward manner, rather than sneaking around.

## Myth: "Geminis Will Always Change Their Opinion for No Reason"

Some folks assume that Geminis shift their stance simply to be contrary or to seek attention. They say Geminis hold no firm beliefs because they are always changing perspectives. In reality, Geminis often gather new facts or hear different arguments, then adjust their opinion based on what they learn.

**Why This Myth Exists**:

**Curiosity**: A Gemini might explore many viewpoints quickly, seeming inconsistent to those who cling to a single opinion.

**Devil's Advocate**: Sometimes, Geminis enjoy playing with possibilities, questioning statements or supporting an opposite view just to see how it stands up.

**Rapid Talks**: The pace of their mental process can look random from the outside.

**The Reality**:

**Information-Based Shifts**: Geminis may change beliefs if presented with strong logic or evidence. This can be a sign of mental flexibility, not confusion.

**Varied Interests**: They might also show passion for multiple sides of a debate, acknowledging the value in each.

**Depth of Thought**: Many Geminis do dig deeper, but from the outside, it might appear like quick flipping if you only catch a snippet of their thought process.

## Myth: "Geminis Cannot Have Deep Relationships"

Because of their social butterfly image, some believe Geminis do not form lasting, meaningful bonds. They assume the Gemini is too scattered to settle into a deep friendship or a long-term partnership. This overlooks the fact that Geminis can be quite caring and devoted once they connect strongly with someone.

**Why This Myth Exists**:

**Multiple Friend Groups**: A Gemini might have acquaintances in many circles, so people see them hopping around socially.

**Shorter Interactions**: Quick chats might make others think Geminis never invest enough time to build depth.

**Tendency to Move**: If Geminis live in different places or shift jobs, some relationships might fade, giving the impression they cannot keep deep ties.

**The Reality**:

**Selective Depth**: Geminis might have a small circle of very close friends or family they trust wholeheartedly, even if they also have many casual contacts.

**Bonding Through Words**: They can share many personal thoughts through long conversations, building emotional closeness with those they trust.

**Creative Support**: Geminis often encourage loved ones' ideas and dreams, showing a real depth of care.

## Myth: "Geminis Are Only Interested in Surface-Level Topics"

People sometimes think Geminis skim across subjects without going into depth. They point to the sign's appetite for quick facts, implying that Geminis do not want deeper knowledge. But in reality, many Geminis love diving deeply into a topic that truly fascinates them.

**Why This Myth Exists:**

**Wider Range of Interests:** Because Geminis jump between subjects, it can look like they never focus on one.

**Trivia Love:** Their enjoyment of random facts might be mistaken for not wanting to learn the substance behind them.

**Fear of Boredom:** They do shift away from dull content, so if a subject is taught in a dry way, they might not stick around.

**The Reality:**

**Niche Deep Dives:** When Geminis find a topic that sparks real curiosity—like technology, psychology, or art—they can spend hours studying it, collecting data, or practicing new skills.

**Progressive Engagement:** They may start with a surface overview, then research deeper layers over time.

**Sharing Knowledge:** Once they gain a deeper understanding, they often share it enthusiastically, showing they can go beyond a shallow level.

## Myth: "Geminis Are Always Jokesters and Never Serious"

Another misunderstanding is that Geminis laugh at everything and cannot handle serious matters. People assume the Gemini approach is to make jokes and avoid responsibility. While Geminis do use humor, they can be highly responsible and serious when necessary.

**Why This Myth Exists:**

**Humor as Connection:** Many Geminis rely on light-hearted banter to bond with others.

**Easing Tension:** They might crack jokes in tense situations, giving the impression they are not taking things seriously.

**The Reality:**

**Knowing When to Be Serious**: Geminis typically read the room. In important moments—like work deadlines, big family issues, or emotional talks—they can step up with focus and calm.

**Humor as a Tool**: They may use humor to defuse conflict or help people relax, not just to avoid adult responsibilities.

**Work Ethic**: Many Geminis excel in demanding jobs. Their adaptability helps them handle tasks effectively, proving they are not all fun and games.

## Myth: "Geminis Are Easily Bored by Everything"

It is said that Geminis get bored so quickly that they cannot enjoy a calm routine or slower-paced activities. While Geminis do value variety, they can find fun in many things, even those that seem slow, if it sparks their mind or offers a new angle.

**Why This Myth Exists:**

**Enthusiasm for Change**: They might talk often about new ideas or experiences, fueling the image that everything else is boring.

**Energy Surges**: Quick excitement can fade if the environment does not feed their curiosity.

**The Reality:**

**Active Observation**: Geminis can find small details interesting—even in a supposedly boring setting—if it captures their attention.

**Self-Entertainment**: Many Geminis keep themselves engaged through daydreams, side thoughts, or noticing patterns. They are not always dependent on external thrills.

**Flexible Routines**: They might adapt a steady schedule, inserting occasional twists or changes to keep it from feeling monotonous.

## Myth: "Geminis Cannot Hold Down Long-Term Jobs"

Because of talk about them getting bored, some think Geminis jump from one job to another. They may believe Geminis lack the staying power for a career that spans years. However, many Geminis do stick with jobs—especially those that allow room for new challenges.

**Why This Myth Exists**:

**Multiple Career Paths**: Some Geminis switch fields early in life, trying to see which path suits them best.

**Desire for Growth**: They move on if they feel stuck with no mental stimulation.

**Reputation Spread**: People notice the Geminis who job-hop, ignoring those who quietly stay in one role.

**The Reality**:

**Commitment to Development**: A Gemini who finds a workplace offering variety—like new projects or roles—can remain for a long time.

**Entrepreneurial Spirit**: Some Geminis start their own ventures, channeling their adaptability into building something that evolves with them.

**Balanced Approach**: Geminis might make changes within a company, shifting positions rather than leaving entirely.

## Myth: "All Geminis Are the Same and Fit the Label Perfectly"

A broad myth about any zodiac sign is assuming everyone born under it is identical in traits and life choices. For Geminis, people might think every single one is a chatterbox who loves to read or fill their home with constant chaos.

**Why This Myth Exists:**

**General Astrology:** Articles or memes reduce signs to a handful of traits, ignoring personal differences.

**Viral Stereotypes:** Online jokes oversimplify the sign for humor, painting all Geminis with the same brush.

**The Reality:**

**Individual Influences:** Culture, family upbringing, and personal experiences shape how each Gemini's traits manifest.

**Birth Charts:** In astrology, people have entire birth charts with many different sign placements, not just their sun sign.

**Personal Variation:** While some Geminis might match typical patterns (loving variety, chatty, curious), others could be quiet or more reserved, with only subtle hints of the common traits.

## Myth: "Geminis Cannot Be Good Leaders"

There is a myth that because Geminis like to learn and talk to everyone, they cannot handle leadership roles that require steady decision-making. Critics say they will keep changing plans or be too busy chatting to guide a team. This overlooks the fact that many Geminis can excel at leadership when they learn to use their communication gifts wisely.

**Why This Myth Exists:**

**Changing Plans:** Observers assume a Gemini boss might switch directions too often, confusing a team.

**Friendliness:** Some believe being friendly means not being firm enough in decisions.

**Multiple Ideas:** They might fear a Gemini leader's mind is too scattered.

**The Reality**:

**Strong Motivators**: Geminis can inspire team members through clear communication, humor, and supportive feedback.

**Adaptable Leadership**: Being able to pivot if a plan does not work out can be a huge advantage, not a flaw.

**Team Building**: Good leaders know how to connect with each person's strengths—a skill Geminis often have due to their social instincts.

## Myth: "Geminis Only Care About Trends, Not Depth"

The idea here is that Geminis follow whatever is popular—fashion, music, or internet memes—without forming real opinions. While Geminis might be among the first to jump on new trends, they can also have well-thought-out reasons for liking them, and they may even create trends themselves.

**Why This Myth Exists**:

**Curiosity About New Things**: Geminis are quick to explore anything labeled "fresh" or "innovative."

**Constant Updates**: They might talk about whatever is happening now, giving the appearance of a short-term attention span.

**The Reality**:

**Making Informed Choices**: Many Geminis read reviews, watch videos, or discuss with friends before embracing a trend.

**Using Trends Creatively**: They might blend trends with personal style, showing deeper thought.

**Long-Term Passions**: Beyond the hype, Geminis often keep certain hobbies or interests for years if they truly enjoy them.

## Myth: "Geminis Love Gossip More Than Facts"

A common myth is that Geminis talk so much they end up spreading rumors, caring more about juicy stories than the truth. Although Geminis do enjoy conversation, they do not necessarily relish gossip or inaccurate information. In fact, many want correct details and do not want to mislead anyone.

**Why This Myth Exists**:

**Talkative Nature**: The chatter can easily be mistaken for gossip.

**Curiosity**: Seeking out stories might lead them to hear rumors.

**Social Environment**: If they have broad networks, they might hear or pass on a lot of news—some of which could be unverified.

**The Reality**:

**Interest in Facts**: A lot of Geminis prefer checking sources to be sure they are not passing on nonsense.

**Sharing vs. Gossiping**: Telling factual, interesting tidbits is different from malicious gossip. Many Geminis focus on fun or helpful information.

**Ethical Boundaries**: They can learn to filter or confirm details before repeating them, especially if rumors might harm someone.

## Myth: "Geminis Are Immature and Never Grow Up"

Because of their playful side, some think Geminis stay forever in a childish mindset. They might be labeled as people who avoid seriousness or adult responsibilities. But Geminis can embrace responsibility when needed; they just keep a youthful curiosity and sense of humor even as they mature.

**Why This Myth Exists**:

**High Energy**: People see Geminis being excited about new things, which can appear childlike.

**Changing Interests**: Switching hobbies resembles a child's approach—trying many things briefly.

**The Reality**:

**Maintaining Fun**: Enjoying playful activities does not mean they cannot handle adult tasks like paying bills or managing a job.

**Areas of Growth**: As they age, Geminis often learn to channel their energy into stable paths, such as long-term careers or family roles, while still keeping a light spirit.

**Balance**: A Gemini can be playful at the right moments and serious when the situation calls for it, showing real maturity.

## Myth: "Geminis Do Not Believe in Deep Morals or Values"

Another mistaken idea is that because Geminis switch views, they have no firm moral code. This myth suggests that they bend their ethics depending on convenience. In truth, many Geminis hold strong core values but stay open to hearing other viewpoints to refine or confirm those values.

**Why This Myth Exists**:

**Listening to Many Sides**: People see them empathizing with different arguments, thinking that means they have no stance.

**Flexible Social Skills**: Geminis often adapt to fit different groups, which can be read as lacking moral firmness.

**The Reality**:

**Thoughtful Principles**: Geminis might form their morals after researching or discussing them from various angles.

**Respectful Debates**: Their readiness to debate or question can be part of how they clarify their values, not a sign of lacking them.

**Actions Over Words**: Geminis may show their ethics through practical deeds rather than just declaring unwavering beliefs.

# Myth: "Geminis Need Constant Attention and Cannot Be Alone"

While Geminis do love interacting with people, it is an overstatement to say they cannot spend time by themselves. They might go through phases of high social engagement, then enjoy solo activities like writing, reading, or daydreaming.

**Why This Myth Exists**:

**Extroverted Image**: Many portrayals show Geminis as the life of the party, implying they need an audience 24/7.

**Group Behavior**: In a crowd, Geminis may seem to crave attention because they chat with many people.

**The Reality**:

**Independent Exploration**: A lot of Geminis enjoy quiet learning or personal projects without an audience.

**Recharging Alone**: Even an outgoing Gemini might appreciate peaceful moments to reflect and gather new ideas.

**Quality vs. Quantity**: They might prefer meaningful engagements to shallow connections, so they do not chase attention for attention's sake.

# Myth: "Geminis Will Never Commit to a Single Lifestyle or Path"

Some people claim that Geminis drift indefinitely, unable to choose a solid path in careers, relationships, or living situations. While it may take time for a Gemini to settle, many eventually pick a direction that allows enough variety to keep them fulfilled.

**Why This Myth Exists**:

**Experimentation Phase**: Young Geminis may try multiple jobs, partners, or places, which can look like a permanent pattern.

**Fear of Missing Out**: They do worry about closing off possibilities, so they explore widely.

**Late Bloomers**: Some Geminis come into their long-term choices later than others, but that is not universal.

**The Reality**:

**Adaptive Settling**: A Gemini might find a role that keeps evolving or a relationship that offers growth, satisfying their love for change.

**Personal Timeline**: Everyone has a different pace. Geminis might decide firmly at 25 or 50—it depends on when they feel ready.

**Staying Open**: Even after committing, a Gemini might keep a side hobby or side travel plans, but that does not mean they are not dedicated to their main life choice.

## Myth: "Geminis Are Bad Listeners"

Linked to the idea that they talk a lot, some believe Geminis cannot listen well or empathize with others' experiences. People might say Geminis only wait for their turn to speak. Yet, a large number of Geminis actually excel at active listening because they crave information and stories.

**Why This Myth Exists**:

**Fast Thinking**: Observers see Geminis rapidly forming answers, missing that they can also retain what the other person says.

**Conversation Shifts**: Jumping from one topic to another might appear as not listening thoroughly.

**The Reality**:

**Information Seeking**: If a Gemini is truly interested, they ask questions and pay attention to details. They want to learn from the speaker.

**Reflective Listening**: Some Geminis use clarifying questions or repeat back key points, showing real engagement.

**When Distracted**: If bored or feeling the topic is stagnant, a Gemini might check out mentally, but that is not the same as being incapable of listening.

## Myth: "Geminis Are Jealous of Every Other Sign"

Occasionally, people will say that Geminis are jealous because other signs might seem more stable or more intense. This myth paints Geminis as insecure about not fitting one single mold. In truth, Geminis often like their unique position, enjoying the mental freedom it brings.

**Why This Myth Exists**:

**Comparisons**: Some see Geminis trying new traits—like a burst of fiery passion or calm stability—and think they envy the signs that naturally exhibit them.

**Stereotype Collisions**: Online zodiac jokes sometimes pit signs against each other, claiming rivalry or jealousy.

**The Reality**:

**Personal Choice**: Many Geminis value their own adaptability, not wishing to be something else.

**Selective Inspiration**: If they see qualities in another sign—like strong determination—they might incorporate it, but that is not jealousy, it is learning.

**Happy with Variety**: Rather than envying stability, Geminis often appreciate that they can adapt or explore multiple sides of life.

## Myth: "Geminis Lack Compassion"

Finally, some claim that Geminis focus so much on intellectual pursuits they fail to show warmth or compassion. They might see Geminis analyzing feelings instead of comforting someone. However, that underestimates the empathy that many Geminis feel and express through conversation, advice, or direct help.

**Why This Myth Exists:**

**Logical Tones**: A Gemini might offer solutions or new viewpoints when someone is upset, which can appear unfeeling if the person just wants emotional support.

**Busy Minds**: In group situations, they might miss cues if they are juggling multiple conversations.

**The Reality:**

**Support Through Words**: Geminis often provide emotional help by talking through problems or sharing personal stories.

**Action-Oriented Kindness**: They might do favors, run errands, or gather resources to help, reflecting genuine concern.

**Awareness Gap**: Some Geminis do need to practice noticing subtle emotional signals, but that does not mean they do not care.

# CHAPTER 17: GEMINI AND CLOSE RELATIONSHIPS

Geminis are often called social butterflies, but there is much more depth to how they connect with friends, family members, and romantic partners. Building strong bonds can be a meaningful part of their lives, even though people might assume that their talkative nature and craving for variety prevent deeper closeness. In truth, Geminis can form some of the most interesting and fulfilling close relationships, as long as they learn to balance their curious spirit with honest commitment. This chapter takes an in-depth look at how Geminis handle close relationships, what they bring to these bonds, and how both Geminis and their loved ones can build mutual trust and affection.

## Openness to Connection

Many Geminis are born conversationalists. They enjoy sharing stories, cracking jokes, and learning about the people around them. This same desire to learn can be a doorway to close bonds. When they meet someone who captures their interest, they ask questions, seek detailed answers, and share personal stories of their own. Over time, such talks can create a strong sense of familiarity.

**Energy in the Early Stages**: In friendships or romantic connections, Geminis often show excitement at the beginning. They may send frequent texts, plan outings, or talk for hours on the phone. This enthusiasm can make new acquaintances feel special and understood.

**Friendship as a Foundation**: Because Geminis value conversation so deeply, they tend to start many close bonds on a friendly note. Even in romantic contexts, they enjoy a partner who can also be a good companion—someone who likes to brainstorm ideas, explore new places, and discuss various subjects.

At the same time, Geminis should be mindful of overwhelming someone with constant chatter or daily messaging. Not everyone moves at that same quick pace. Balancing their eagerness with the other person's comfort level is crucial in nurturing a stable relationship from the start.

## Shared Interests vs. Exploring Differences

Close relationships often develop around shared experiences or common ground. Geminis love discovering mutual interests, whether that is a hobby, a favorite type of music, or a fun topic they can discuss. However, they also appreciate differences, because it gives them something new to learn from their loved one.

### Bonding Through Similarities

**Team Projects**: If both parties enjoy cooking, they might set up cooking nights. This cooperative activity satisfies a Gemini's love for conversation as they chop veggies and debate recipes.

**Creative Ventures**: Two friends or partners who share a passion for art, gaming, or any other pastime can spend hours talking about it, swapping tips and fueling each other's curiosity.

### Embracing Contrasts

**Teaching Each Other**: A Gemini might be fascinated by a partner's unusual career or unique hobby. They ask questions, try it themselves, and find delight in understanding a different world.

**Open-Minded Exchanges**: Because Geminis can handle multiple perspectives, they are often open to someone who has a different background or viewpoint. They see these differences as valuable expansions of their own knowledge.

This blend of similarities and differences can keep the relationship fresh. Geminis thrive on variety, so having a partner or close friend with distinct skills or perspectives can be a plus—rather than a point of conflict.

# Communication: The Heart of Gemini Bonds

Since Geminis are widely recognized for communication talents, it is no surprise that talking and listening are pillars of their close relationships. They want to feel free to express ideas, but they also need to practice active listening to avoid dominating conversations.

**Ways Geminis Strengthen Communication:**

**Asking Thoughtful Questions**: A Gemini who cares about someone will try to uncover deeper layers, going beyond surface-level facts.

**Sharing Personal Thoughts**: While Geminis can be chatty, they sometimes dodge heavier emotions. Once they trust someone, they might reveal more personal feelings or vulnerabilities, which deepens the bond.

**Encouraging Openness**: In a friend group or partnership, Geminis may break awkward silences with lighthearted jokes or by prompting others to share their viewpoints.

**Challenges to Watch Out For:**

**Talking Over Others**: If a Gemini becomes excited, they might cut in before the other person finishes, accidentally sending the message that they are not interested in listening.

**Jumping Topics Too Fast**: Rapid topic changes can leave a friend or partner struggling to keep up, especially if the conversation moves from one idea to the next without closure.

**Over-Reliance on Words**: While talking is great, people sometimes need silent empathy. Geminis can work on providing comfort through simple presence if a loved one is upset, rather than responding with quick solutions or shifting the conversation.

# Trust and Loyalty

A stereotype about Gemini is that they struggle with loyalty. It is true that their desire for newness can lead them to explore many connections, but once they find someone they genuinely click with, they can be quite loyal. However, trust in a Gemini relationship might hinge on openness and mental compatibility more than typical signs of devotion.

**Building Trust with Gemini:**

**Honest Discussions**: Geminis generally respect directness. If they sense hidden agendas, they may feel uneasy. Being clear about issues or worries goes a long way toward earning their loyalty.

**Mental Connection**: For Geminis, part of trust is knowing they can share random thoughts or unusual opinions without being judged. Feeling mentally accepted fosters loyalty.

**Balanced Freedom**: Geminis remain loyal when they do not feel trapped. Giving them personal space to explore hobbies, friendships, or solo outings can reduce any temptation to pull away.

**Possible Pitfalls**:

**Jealousy from Others**: A partner or friend might question why Geminis talk to so many people or have wide social circles, leading to misunderstandings if not addressed calmly.

**Gemini's Own Temptation**: If a Gemini is bored in a relationship with no intellectual spark, they may drift toward something more interesting. That is less about disloyalty and more about unfulfilled mental needs.

Maintaining trust in close bonds thus relies on satisfying these needs for honest talk, mental stimulation, and a degree of independence, all balanced with emotional warmth.

## Emotional Intimacy and Vulnerability

Though Geminis are known for logic and words, they do experience deep emotions. Emotional intimacy can grow when they feel safe sharing. Yet, they might hesitate if they worry the other person will not "get" them or if they fear coming across as overly serious. Encouraging a Gemini to open up at a deeper emotional level can be key in forging a tight bond.

**Indicators a Gemini Feels Safe**:

**Speaking About Fears or Past Hurts**: If they dare to mention childhood struggles, insecurities, or mistakes, it shows real trust.

**Seeking Solace**: A Gemini who normally tries to solve problems logically might let a close friend or partner console them, indicating they are comfortable revealing raw feelings.

**Less Showy, More Genuine**: In public, Geminis may lighten the mood with jokes. In private, they may drop the funny act and talk plainly about what is on their heart.

**How to Help a Gemini Open Up**:

**Be a Good Listener**: Avoid interrupting or giving immediate advice. Let them talk through the details.

**Validate Emotions**: Show that their feelings are normal and not a burden.

**Stay Patient**: Geminis can switch subjects if they feel awkward. Gently circling back when they are ready can encourage deeper connection over time.

This emotional dimension adds another layer to Gemini relationships—beyond fun banter and intellectual chatter—to include real empathy and closeness.

## Gemini in Romantic Relationships

Many people wonder how Geminis behave as romantic partners. The short answer is that they bring excitement, spontaneity, and mental stimulation to a romance. However, they also need a partner who can keep up with their evolving interests and who will not panic if the Gemini suggests something offbeat.

**Romantic Strengths**:

**Playful Courtship**: Flirting might feel easy for Geminis, who can charm a partner with humor and quick thinking. Dates might involve exploring new restaurants, trying silly games, or going to unusual local events.

**Steady Communication**: Partners rarely wonder what is on a Gemini's mind, because they often speak up.

**Innovation in the Relationship**: To keep things fresh, Geminis propose spontaneous getaways, shared hobbies, or a new way of doing daily routines.

**Common Concerns**:

**Need for Independence**: They do not like feeling fenced in. If the relationship has too many rules or tight restrictions, they might pull away.

**Inconsistency**: The partner might feel confused if the Gemini's mood flips from sweet and engaging to distant or aloof the next day. This is not always about losing interest—sometimes Geminis need personal mental space.

**Handling Boredom**: Long-term relationships demand more than initial sparks. Geminis benefit from building shared goals or projects to maintain interest.

For Geminis, romance is a chance to share mental synergy with a loved one. As they settle into a stable bond, they often see it less as "being tied down" and more as "having a companion to explore life's possibilities." With open dialogue, they can handle the natural ups and downs of love.

## Gemini in Family Settings

Geminis typically bring a lively spirit to family life, whether as a parent, child, or sibling. They are often the ones sparking group discussions, suggesting new holiday activities, or encouraging everyone to try something different. Yet, they also need acceptance of their changing moods or interests within the family.

**Parent-Child Dynamics**:

**As Children**: A Gemini child might ask endless questions, want varied after-school clubs, and get bored if forced to do the same thing every day. Parents who embrace these curiosities can help the Gemini child thrive.

**As Parents**: A Gemini parent might introduce kids to many books or games, encouraging mental exploration. They often chat easily with their children, bridging age gaps through playful talks. However, they must watch for times the child needs consistent routines and emotional steadiness.

**Handling Family Conflicts**:

**Talking it Out**: Geminis might use reason to solve family arguments, pointing out solutions or listing pros and cons. Family members who prefer a direct emotional approach could interpret this as detachment, so Geminis may need to tune in to feelings more.

**Adapting to Changes**: If the family relocates or experiences big events, Geminis may adapt quicker than others, but they should remember not everyone adjusts at that same pace.

Overall, a Gemini can be a source of fun ideas and open dialogues in a family, as long as they respect the group's need for stability.

# Gemini as a Friend

When it comes to friendships, Geminis might appear to have a wide social circle. They often chat comfortably with neighbors, classmates, or coworkers, gathering a broad range of acquaintances. However, deeper friendships form when a Gemini truly connects mentally or emotionally with someone.

**Signs of True Friendship with a Gemini**:

**Long Conversations**: They stay on the phone or chat apps for extended periods, happily discussing anything.

**Invitations to Special Activities**: Whether it is a small event or a bigger trip, a Gemini who consistently invites a friend is showing real fondness.

**Inside Jokes and References**: A hallmark of close Gemini friendships is remembering little details or jokes they share, forging a sense of belonging.

**Maintaining Friendship**:

**Check In**: Geminis can get swept up in new interests, so sending a friendly message if they vanish for a while helps. Most Geminis appreciate these reminders that someone cares.

**Allow Flexibility**: Pushing a Gemini friend into strict routines, like "We must meet every Thursday at exactly 6 PM," can feel stifling. Instead, they do better with more open plans.

**Shared Curiosity**: Doing novel activities together—visiting an odd museum, attending a unique workshop—feeds the fun. It keeps the friendship from going stale.

Though Geminis may have multiple friend groups, they typically remain loyal to the ones who understand their multifaceted personality. They value people who let them explore different sides of themselves without judgment.

## Conflict and Resolution

No matter how strong the bond, disagreements can arise in relationships with Geminis. Possible triggers include the Gemini's sudden plan changes, blunt observations, or perceived inconsistency. However, Geminis can also excel at resolving disputes if they use their communication skills wisely.

**Common Conflict Triggers**:

**Mixed Signals**: A friend or partner may be unsure what the Gemini truly wants if they share contradictory statements in a short time.

**Feeling Ignored**: Sometimes, Geminis focus on new people or tasks, leaving an existing friend or partner feeling neglected.

**Pushing Personal Boundaries**: The Gemini may press for details or opinions about sensitive topics, not realizing the other person is uncomfortable.

**Healthy Ways to Resolve:**

**Slow Down**: Geminis should listen carefully to the grievance instead of instantly offering five solutions. Letting the other person express their emotions fully is crucial.

**Confirm Understanding**: Repeating what the other person said, in their own words, shows the Gemini comprehends the issue. This step is called reflective listening and can ease tension.

**Work on a Compromise**: Geminis are good at brainstorming. They can propose multiple possible solutions, then let the other person pick or refine one that works best for everyone.

**Acknowledge Feelings**: Logic alone may not solve emotional pain. Geminis can remind themselves to validate how someone feels—even if they do not share the same emotional response.

When used carefully, these communication strengths can turn conflicts into productive discussions rather than ongoing tension.

## Balancing Freedom and Closeness

One challenge for Geminis in close relationships is the need for independence. They can love someone deeply but still crave personal space to explore new ideas or meet new people. At times, this can create misunderstandings if a friend or partner expects constant closeness or a rigid schedule.

**Ways to Balance:**

**Agree on Boundaries**: For a romantic relationship, the pair might agree on how often they want to go out together or how much alone time each needs per week.

**Scheduled "Date Times" or "Friend Times"**: Even if Geminis do not like rigid structure, having set plans on certain days can reassure loved ones while still leaving the rest of the week flexible.

**Communicate About Changes**: If a Gemini must shift a plan, letting others know early and explaining the reason shows respect. That helps reduce the "flaky" label often attached to them.

In friendships, it might look like texting a buddy to say, "I need a quiet weekend to recharge, but let's meet next week." This blend of honesty and courtesy can keep the bond steady.

## Long-Distance Bonds

Because of their comfortable relationship with technology and love of conversation, Geminis can maintain long-distance friendships or romances relatively well—at least for a time. They see video chats, messages, and phone calls as chances to keep the spark alive. However, they also value in-person spontaneity, which can be missing in long-distance settings.

**Strengths in Long-Distance**:

**Creative Communication**: They might send digital postcards, funny voice notes, or short videos about their daily life.

**Mental Connection**: Reading the same eBook or streaming the same show, then discussing it, satisfies a Gemini's desire for shared activity.

**Appreciating Independence**: Long-distance relationships can give them personal space while still keeping a bond.

**Potential Hurdles**:

**Physical Absence**: A Gemini who thrives on face-to-face experiences might find it tough not to share daily adventures in person.

**Staying Consistent**: Because Geminis can change their routine or get lost in local social circles, they might neglect scheduled calls if not careful.

**Missing Spontaneity**: They cannot spontaneously pop by a friend's home or plan a quick outing together if they live far apart, which can dampen a Gemini's sense of fun.

Successful long-distance ties often rely on planning virtual meetups, sending small updates, and occasionally traveling to see one another in person.

## Growing with a Gemini

Long-term relationships with a Gemini—whether as a best friend or life partner—can evolve significantly over time. Because Geminis themselves grow by picking up new interests, the dynamic may shift. Loved ones can find this exciting if they share that sense of curiosity or are open to changes.

**Phases in the Relationship**:

**Early Spark**: The Gemini's lively curiosity draws people in. They might fill days with chatting, exploring, and forming an instant bond.

**Settling Down**: As they get comfortable, Geminis show deeper sides, discussing personal dreams and working through bigger life decisions.

**Expansion**: Over years, they might propose unexpected ideas—like relocating, starting a joint venture, or adopting new hobbies together. The relationship can keep adapting if both parties are flexible.

**Encouraging Mutual Growth**:

**Share Future Goals**: If the relationship is heading toward serious commitment, talking about upcoming milestones—like buying a home, traveling abroad, or personal achievements—can keep both sides aligned.

**Check In**: Regularly asking each other, "Are we both enjoying where this is going?" helps ensure that new directions remain exciting, not alienating.

## Handling the Gemini "Dual Nature"

Many references to Gemini mention a "dual nature," usually symbolized by twins. Loved ones might worry that this implies unpredictability. In a close relationship, "dual nature" can simply mean that Geminis can shift from playful to thoughtful quickly, or that they see multiple angles to a problem.

**Positive Use of Dual Nature**:

**Problem-Solving**: A Gemini who sees two sides may negotiate between them, helping couples or friends find middle ground.

**Adaptation**: If circumstances change—a job is lost, or a friend moves away—Geminis can pivot to new plans more easily, offering reassurance.

**Emotional Range**: While some interpret changing moods as a negative, it can also be a sign of emotional flexibility. They do not get stuck in one feeling too long, and they might help a friend shift perspective when upset.

**Caution**:

**Unclear Signals**: Because Geminis can flip from serious to joking, or from calm to energetic, a partner might get confused if they are not used to these switches.

**Needing Stability**: Even though Geminis manage change well, some major life transitions still require a consistent approach. They should remember that not everyone in the relationship changes at the same speed.

## Common Missteps and How to Fix Them

Even the most self-aware Gemini can slip up in close relationships. Recognizing these typical mistakes and handling them positively can save or strengthen the bond.

**Overbooking Social Plans**: A Gemini might say yes to two invites on the same day, leading to a no-show or rushed appearances at both events.

**Fix**: Apologize sincerely, explain the scheduling clash, and propose a fresh plan or time to make it up.

**Forgetting Emotional Support**: Sometimes, they might address a friend's or partner's problem too rationally, skipping the comfort that person needs.

**Fix**: Slow down, express empathy, and ask, "Do you want me to listen, or do you want ideas?" This question can clarify what kind of support is needed.

**Ignoring Boredom Warnings**: If the relationship or friendship starts feeling stale, a Gemini might drift away without discussing it.

**Fix**: Bring up the topic politely: "I've noticed we're stuck in the same routine. How about we find something new to try together?" This approach can refresh the bond.

Taking responsibility and adjusting behaviors can demonstrate the genuine care that many Geminis feel but may occasionally fail to show in the right way.

## Strategies for Loved Ones

Those who are close to Geminis can also play a role in making the relationship thrive. Understanding how to handle the Gemini's energy can prevent misunderstandings.

**Appreciate Their Enthusiasm**: If they ramble excitedly about a new hobby, show genuine interest or at least let them share for a moment. Dismissing them can make them feel unvalued.

**Encourage Without Cornering**: Suggest interesting activities or ask for the Gemini's input, but avoid pushing them if they are in a quiet mood. Striking that balance respects their free-spirited side.

**Give Gentle Reminders**: If you sense they might forget an important plan or detail, kindly check in beforehand. Geminis often appreciate a friendly nudge rather than a scolding.

## Sustaining Long-Term Harmony

Staying connected with a Gemini over many years can be a rewarding experience. It allows both sides to witness each other's growth, expansions, and changing interests. But it also demands flexibility, curiosity, and a willingness to adapt to new directions.

**Recurring Checkpoints**: Having a monthly or quarterly "talk session" where each person openly shares what is going on in their life can keep the bond fresh.

**Joint Adventures**: Whether it is traveling to a new place once a year or signing up for a local workshop, tackling new challenges together can feed the Gemini's love for novelty while reinforcing unity.

**Respecting Traditions**: Oddly enough, even though Geminis like change, some small traditions—like an annual gathering or a unique holiday ritual—can become cherished landmarks, giving a sense of continuity that helps ground the ever-shifting energies.

## Growth Opportunities in Conflict

When a Gemini relationship faces a serious test—perhaps a breach of trust or a heavy life event—both sides can either break apart or use the conflict as a route to deeper understanding. Geminis, being open to learning, may come out of tough times with more maturity if they handle conflicts with honesty and willingness to improve.

**Steps for Personal Growth**:

**Self-Reflection**: Recognizing their own missteps in the conflict, not just blaming the other person.

**Accepting Feedback**: If loved ones point out a Gemini's pattern—like always interrupting or forgetting emotional cues—the Gemini can take note and change.

**Integration**: After resolution, they can integrate lessons learned into daily habits. For instance, scheduling fewer but higher-quality meetups if over-scheduling was the issue.

Such challenges, when met, often tighten the bond because both Gemini and their friend or partner see a real commitment to growth and empathy.

# Friends and Partners from Different Signs

Although this book focuses on Gemini traits, it helps to note that any sign can bond with a Gemini, given understanding and mutual respect. Some relationships might be more straightforward—like with fellow air signs who enjoy mental exploration—while others can be a bit more complementary, such as with earth signs that offer stability.

**Harmonizing Styles**:

**Air Sign Friends (Libra, Aquarius)**: They share intellectual sparks, talk for hours, and appreciate big-picture thinking. Potential risk: staying in the realm of ideas too much, ignoring practical steps.

**Fire Signs (Aries, Leo, Sagittarius)**: They match Gemini's energy and spontaneity, but conflicts may arise if both sides want to be the main spark of attention.

**Water Signs (Cancer, Scorpio, Pisces)**: Water signs bring emotional depth, balancing Gemini's logic. Friction can come from differences in communication speed or emotional processing.

**Earth Signs (Taurus, Virgo, Capricorn)**: Earth signs add grounding, helping Geminis structure their lives. Tensions might occur if the earth sign wants more consistency than the Gemini can provide.

Each pairing has its pros and cons, but with open minds, Geminis can form meaningful bonds across the entire zodiac spectrum.

# Maintaining Equality in the Relationship

Whether in friendships or romance, Geminis do best in a setting of equality—where both parties share ideas and decisions. They prefer not to feel dominated or to dominate someone else. Because they can argue persuasively, they should watch out for accidentally overshadowing a quieter friend or partner.

**Encouraging Balanced Dynamics**:

**Invite Input**: A Gemini can ask, "What do you think?" to ensure the other person's voice is heard.

**Rotate Leadership**: In group tasks or shared living situations, they can take turns deciding what to do, ensuring one side does not control everything.

**Notice Nonverbal Cues**: If the other person looks uneasy or tries to speak but is interrupted, the Gemini can pause and let them share properly.

This approach builds trust and mutual respect, countering any concern that the relationship is too Gemini-centered.

## When Relationships End

Not all bonds last, and sometimes a Gemini connection breaks due to shifting interests, conflicts, or life changes. Geminis might handle endings in a direct way, explaining their reasons and moving on. However, it can still be a painful process—especially if there was deep emotional investment.

**Typical Ending Patterns**:

**Fade-Out**: The Gemini might drift from someone if they sense no more growth or shared enjoyment. This can cause confusion if not communicated clearly.

**Honest Conversation**: A more self-aware Gemini will try to talk it through, expressing what changed or why they feel the bond cannot continue.

**Remaining Friendly**: They might offer to stay on good terms, though it depends on the nature of the split. Some can remain acquaintances who chat occasionally, reflecting the Gemini desire to keep connections intact if possible.

It can help for both sides to see the ending not as betrayal but as a recognition that the relationship dynamic no longer serves them both. The Gemini approach is often forward-looking, focusing on what they have learned and what comes next.

## Special Challenges with Introverted Loved Ones

If a Gemini is close to a person who is more introverted, conflicts can arise when the Gemini wants frequent contact and the introverted individual needs more space. Navigating this difference with respect ensures the relationship remains respectful to each style.

**Adjusting to Different Social Needs**:

**Slow the Pace**: The Gemini can send a message to check if the friend or partner is up for a call or outing, rather than spontaneously showing up.

**Offer Calm Hobbies**: Instead of always pushing group gatherings, try quieter meetups—like reading in the same space or going for a peaceful walk.

**Communication Clarity**: If the introvert needs alone time, Geminis should not take it personally, but see it as normal recharging.

Learning each other's rhythms can prevent misunderstandings that might break an otherwise solid bond.

## Support Through Life Changes

Geminis might excel at offering mental solutions when loved ones face life shifts, such as job changes, losses, or health issues. However, they can also show support through small acts, not just words.

**Being There**:

**Check-Ins**: A quick call or text asking, "How are things today?" can reassure someone going through a tough phase.

**Practical Help**: Running errands, helping research solutions, or introducing them to relevant contacts can lighten the load.

**Listening Mode**: Sometimes, a friend or partner simply needs to vent. Geminis can strive to be patient even if their mind wants to jump in with suggestions.

This approach makes them valuable companions in both fun and challenging times.

## Appreciating Gemini's Liveliness and Depth

Despite the myths, close relationships with Geminis can be remarkable. Their lively presence brings color, conversation, and unique ways of handling daily routines. Friends, family, and partners often note that life feels less dull with a Gemini around. Meanwhile, Geminis appreciate companions who offer them acceptance, gentle stability, and a bit of adventure.

**Signs a Gemini Relationship Is Flourishing**:

**Shared Laughter**: Jokes and playful banter flow easily, but do not overshadow important topics.

**Growth Mindset**: Both sides support each other's personal development and do not resist the other's need to try new things.

**Open Discourse**: Issues are talked through without fear. The Gemini feels comfortable discussing confusion or shifts in perspective.

# CHAPTER 18: FAMOUS GEMINIS

Geminis have shaped many fields—from entertainment to science, politics, and beyond. While a single zodiac sign does not automatically grant greatness, the Gemini traits of curiosity, adaptability, and strong communication can coincide with remarkable achievements. This chapter explores well-known figures often linked with Gemini birthdays, illustrating how some typical Gemini qualities might have played a role in their paths. We will look at historical, artistic, and contemporary examples, bearing in mind that each individual is unique and shaped by far more than just their sun sign.

Please note: Exact birth times and dates can vary by source, and not everyone believes in astrology. Still, we can have fun exploring how these public figures might reflect certain Gemini traits in their lives and careers.

## Historical Leaders and Explorers

Throughout history, some leaders, explorers, and inventors recognized as Geminis have displayed strong communication, curiosity, and willingness to adapt to challenges. Let's look at a few who have been frequently associated with this sign (acknowledging that historical birth records can be less precise).

**Jean-Paul Marat (Born May 24, 1743)**: A figure of the French Revolution, Marat was known for his writings and fiery journalism. Though his style was controversial, he influenced the course of the revolution with passionate articles and strong opinions.

**Gemini Traits**: Quick thinking in debates and a talent for written communication. His pamphlets stirred the public's emotions and spread revolutionary ideas rapidly.

**John F. Kennedy (Born May 29, 1917)**: The 35th President of the United States, famous for his speeches and charismatic leadership style.

**Gemini Traits**: Kennedy's oratory skill, his push for new ideas like the space program ("We choose to go to the moon"), and his ability to connect with diverse groups reflect qualities often tied to Gemini—bold vision, adaptability, and strong communication.

**Sir Arthur Conan Doyle (Born May 22, 1859)**: While not an explorer in the literal sense, Conan Doyle, the creator of Sherlock Holmes, explored detective fiction in a groundbreaking way.

**Gemini Traits**: Masterful at weaving complex plots, swiftly switching readers' perspectives, and using rational problem-solving that reflects a sharp Gemini mind at work.

Such historical figures are often marked by their vocal presence, adaptability to political or social shifts, and a thirst for new ideas. Their Gemini side may show up in how they used language or how they responded to evolving challenges, though each person's life story is more complex than any zodiac label.

## Literary Giants

Some of the world's most famous authors, poets, and playwrights fall under the Gemini time frame. Their works frequently reveal mental agility, playful language, or intricate narrative structures that keep audiences engaged.

**Walt Whitman (Born May 31, 1819)**: An iconic American poet, best known for *Leaves of Grass*.

**Gemini Traits**: Embracing the vastness of human experience, shifting between personal reflection and universal themes, and presenting an innovative style that broke from traditional forms. Whitman's free verse approach and constant revisions hint at a mind restless for improvement and variety.

**Thomas Hardy (Born June 2, 1840)**: Although best known for novels that explore tragic themes, Hardy also displayed a versatile approach to writing, producing poetry and short stories alongside his famous novels.

**Gemini Traits**: Skilled at depicting rural life and human emotions in detail, Hardy's ability to inhabit multiple perspectives in his narratives might reflect the duality of the sign.

**Ian Fleming (Born May 28, 1908)**: The creator of James Bond.

**Gemini Traits**: Bond's world of espionage features quick wit, excitement, and shifting settings—factors that might echo the Gemini love of adventure and mental sparks. Fleming's writing style is both direct and imaginative, swinging from everyday details to exotic locales.

These literary figures often changed styles or tackled varied subjects, demonstrating curiosity that would not be confined to a single genre or topic. The adaptability and verbal prowess sometimes ascribed to Gemini might be found in their flexible writing methods or the way they constantly pushed their craft forward.

## Music Icons

Music is another domain where Geminis have left a considerable mark. Whether through pop, rock, or classical, many Gemini artists captivate audiences with original expression and an ability to shift styles.

**Paul McCartney (Born June 18, 1942)**: A founding member of The Beatles, one of the most influential bands in history.

**Gemini Traits**: Known for musical innovation, McCartney has tried numerous genres—rock, pop, classical compositions, and more—reflecting the Gemini capacity to explore fresh ideas. His songwriting partnership with John Lennon also shows how Geminis thrive when exchanging ideas with equally creative minds.

**Kanye West (Born June 8, 1977)**: A hip-hop producer and rapper widely recognized for his constant reinvention of style and controversial yet attention-grabbing public persona.

**Gemini Traits**: Shifting musical directions over the years, strong communication (though sometimes divisive), and an outspoken nature that stirs dialogue—be it admiration or debate.

**Laurie Anderson (Born June 5, 1947)**: An experimental musician and performance artist known for blending storytelling, electronics, and visual art in her works.

**Gemini Traits**: Innovative, crossing boundaries between musical genres, spoken word, and theater, which aligns with Gemini's flexible approach to creative endeavors and fascination with multiple forms of expression.

From rock legends to experimental creators, these Gemini musicians often stand out for switching up their sounds, merging influences, or combining conversation-like lyrics with musical artistry.

## Film and Theater Stars

In acting and film, Geminis sometimes shine because they can slip into different characters or handle complex dialogue with ease. Their natural expressiveness and quick wits suit the demands of performing arts.

**Marilyn Monroe (Born June 1, 1926)**: A Hollywood icon recognized for her comedic roles, glamour, and public persona that alternated between bubbly innocence and clever wit.

**Gemini Traits**: On-screen, she displayed charm and comedic timing. Off-screen, she read widely and sometimes wrestled with deeper personal issues, hinting at the Gemini contrast between playful public image and private reflection.

**Morgan Freeman (Born June 1, 1937)**: Esteemed for his deep voice and thoughtful presence across various film genres.

**Gemini Traits**: Demonstrates strong communication and a calm yet adaptable acting range. He can play comedic, dramatic, and authoritative roles, shifting seamlessly between them.

**Natalie Portman (Born June 9, 1981)**: An award-winning actress known for tackling roles that range from blockbusters to intense character studies.

**Gemini Traits**: Skilled at balancing mainstream appeal with academically challenging pursuits (she studied at a top university). Her on-screen roles often show versatility and depth, reflecting the Gemini thirst for mental challenges.

These stars highlight adaptability in portraying multiple personas, navigating different genres, and engaging with audiences in a way that resonates with Gemini's social flair and intellectual range.

## Sports Figures

Not all Geminis are artists or politicians—some excel in sports, where mental agility, quick reactions, and the ability to switch tactics fast can be valuable. The sign's inclination to adapt can lead to success in fast-paced sporting events.

**Venus Williams (Born June 17, 1980)**: A tennis champion recognized for her powerful playing style and strategic thinking on the court.

**Gemini Traits**: Quick reflexes, ability to read opponents' tactics, and resilience under changing match conditions. Off the court, she has ventured into business and fashion lines, showing typical Gemini broad interests.

**Allen Iverson (Born June 7, 1975)**: A basketball legend remembered for his incredible ball-handling skills and fearless style.

**Gemini Traits**: Known for improvisational moves on the court, frequently changing direction to outmaneuver defenders—fitting the sign's fast mind and willingness to try bold plays.

**Novak Djokovic (Born May 22, 1987)**: Another tennis star who has been at the top of the sport for many years, known for his mental tenacity and varied playing style.

**Gemini Traits**: Constantly evolving technique, strategic versatility, and strong communication with fans. He also shows humor and charm in interviews, typical of the sign's social side.

In these sports icons, the twin energies may manifest as an ability to pivot quickly or adapt strategies mid-game, as well as being vocal about their beliefs—qualities that keep them in the spotlight both during matches and in the public arena.

## Science and Innovation

Gemini's trait of seeking new information can fit scientific minds, as they devour research, shift approaches based on data, and communicate their findings well. While precise birth data can be unclear for some historical scientists, several notable figures are often listed as Gemini.

**Rachel Carson (Born May 27, 1907)**: An American marine biologist whose writings on environmental issues, particularly the impact of pesticides, sparked a global movement.

**Gemini Traits**: Her ability to transform scientific findings into clear, persuasive text that resonated with the public highlights the communication hallmark of the sign. She also adjusted her perspective based on new environmental data, showcasing open-mindedness.

**Sally Ride (Born May 26, 1951)**: The first American woman in space. Ride was also known for encouraging STEM education among young students, especially girls.

**Gemini Traits**: Curiosity and adaptability are central to being an astronaut. Ride had strong communication skills, helping the public understand space travel. She later wrote children's science books, a typical Gemini approach: bridging information and storytelling.

Their achievements point to a willingness to question established norms and share discoveries with wide audiences—a communication drive that helps shape public understanding.

## Contemporary Influencers and Entrepreneurs

In the modern age of social media and tech-driven lifestyles, Geminis continue to appear among influential entrepreneurs and innovators. Their comfort with rapid changes can suit them well in industries where trends shift every few months.

**Awkwafina (Nora Lum, Born June 2, 1988)**: An actress, rapper, and comedian. She gained recognition through social media videos before entering mainstream films and television.

**Gemini Traits**: Blending comedic rap, acting, and comedic writing, she crosses multiple entertainment realms. Her online presence and easy rapport with fans reflect Gemini's adaptability and lively communication.

**Angelina Jolie (Born June 4, 1975)**: While primarily known as an actress, she has also engaged in humanitarian work and directed films.

**Gemini Traits**: A career spanning many roles, from acting in big-budget action to more serious dramas, plus a broad personal life that includes adopting children from different countries. Her willingness to speak on global issues might mirror a Gemini's tendency to voice opinions and stand for causes.

Entrepreneurs, influencers, or multi-talented personalities often exhibit a swirl of creative, communicative, and flexible behavior that can align with Gemini traits—though, as always, each individual's story goes beyond simple star sign definitions.

## Musical Theater and Stage Performers

Geminis in the theater world often excel at improvisation, comedic timing, and dynamic acting or singing styles that shift from role to role. Their mental agility can help them memorize lines, adapt to changes mid-performance, and maintain lively interactions with the audience.

**Patti LaBelle (Born May 24, 1944)**: A legendary soul singer known for her powerful voice and stage presence.

**Gemini Traits**: Long career, willingness to experiment with different musical genres, and an ability to connect with fans, constantly reinventing stage costumes and setlists.

**Judy Garland (Born June 10, 1922)**: A Hollywood and theater icon, best known for her role as Dorothy in *The Wizard of Oz* and her outstanding vocal performances.

**Gemini Traits**: Balancing film, concert tours, and stage acts, she showcased adaptability. Her emotional expression in songs and comedic timing in certain roles hinted at a rich emotional range behind the scenes.

Stage or screen, many Gemini performers show the unique knack for stepping into varied characters or persona changes, fueled by their capacity for rapid shifts in creative direction.

## Dynamic Writers and Journalists

Beyond fiction authors, Geminis appear among journalists, critics, or essayists who excel at breaking down complex topics for large audiences. Their investigative side can combine with expressive writing to produce influential works.

**Anne Frank (Born June 12, 1929)**: Known worldwide for *The Diary of a Young Girl*, written while hiding from the Nazis during World War II.

**Gemini Traits**: Even in extremely difficult circumstances, she showed a bright, curious mind in her writings—reflecting on the world around her, pondering human nature, and finding small joys. Her direct, honest style resonates powerfully to this day.

**Joan Rivers (Born June 8, 1933)**: While known primarily as a comedian, she was also a writer, creating books and comedic scripts that dissected social norms.

**Gemini Traits**: Sharp tongue and quick retorts, plus a constant push to rework her material. She had a prolific career spanning stand-up, talk shows, and red carpet hosting, reflecting a typical Gemini restlessness for fresh angles.

Their voices often stand out for the clarity and energy in their writing, aimed at communicating something thought-provoking or entertaining.

Whether comedic or deeply reflective, these skills mirror the Gemini love of words and variety.

## Maintaining a Balanced View

While it is exciting to connect certain personalities with Gemini traits, it is vital to remember that success or recognition does not hinge on astrology alone. The environment in which these individuals grew up, the opportunities they had, their personal drive, and countless other factors shaped their achievements.

**Individual Variations**: Two people with the same birthday can turn out very differently due to life choices and circumstances.

**Other Birth Chart Factors**: Moon sign, rising sign, and planet placements can all influence how Gemini qualities manifest, leading to different styles of expression.

**Shared Patterns, Not Proof**: While we see recurring themes—like adaptability, skillful communication, or a love for switching styles—these alone do not explain someone's entire path to fame.

Still, it is intriguing to see how many noted figures associated with Gemini have, in one way or another, displayed patterns of versatility, openness to learning, and a knack for engaging with the public. It highlights how the sign's strengths—when developed—can lead to memorable contributions in various fields.

## Embracing Complexity

One reason so many Geminis appear in creative or public roles might be their willingness to handle multiple viewpoints and quickly adapt to changing situations. Actors choose different roles, politicians address varied audiences, and writers shift narrative voices. This resonates with the sign's symbol of twins, reflecting multiple facets of personality.

**Freedom to Explore**: A lot of successful Geminis mention how they refused to be confined by one label. They tried new approaches—writing in different genres, playing many roles, or speaking about numerous issues.

**Balancing Act**: Some got criticized for seeming contradictory or unpredictable. However, fans often praise them for refusing to stay stuck in one box.

**Continuous Reinvention**: Revising style, turning to new mediums, or changing the public image is common among Geminis. Their fans might be surprised at each step, but that surprise keeps them in the limelight.

## Lessons from Famous Geminis

People looking to glean insight from these examples might learn several key lessons:

**Stay Curious**: Many Gemini icons never stopped learning or exploring, whether that meant picking up a new instrument, entering a different film genre, or launching a bold initiative.

**Use Words Effectively**: Strong communication—speeches, interviews, lyrics, or books—often propelled these figures into prominence. Honing verbal expression is a powerful tool.

**Embrace Change**: Instead of fearing changes in personal style or shifting career directions, they leveraged those changes to remain fresh and relevant.

**Take Risks**: Gemini boldness can manifest as taking leaps into unfamiliar territory, whether in politics, music, or business. While risk can lead to failure, it can also spark breakthroughs.

## Controversies and Dual Reactions

Some Geminis in the public eye have courted controversy or faced intense scrutiny. The same qualities that spark creativity—like speaking candidly, jumping into new endeavors, or changing stances—can also draw criticism from the public or media.

**Polarizing Figures**: With strong communication, a Gemini might sway fans passionately one way, while angering detractors who see them as inconsistent or confrontational.

**Need for Grounding**: A lesson from certain controversial Gemini figures is that if they do not maintain some grounding—like close advisors or a stable personal life—they might veer into chaos.

**Handling Backlash**: Some respond to negative press with quick wit or explanations, showcasing resilience. Others double down on their positions, sparking further debate.

This dual reaction from the public underscores that the very traits that lead to fame can also create drama.

## International Perspectives

Geminis are found everywhere, across all cultures and professions. While Western media often highlights Hollywood or American politics, global examples abound:

**Che Guevara (Born June 14, 1928)**: Argentine Marxist revolutionary involved in the Cuban Revolution.

**Gemini Traits**: Known for traveling extensively across Latin America in his youth, deeply studying political ideologies, and adapting revolutionary tactics. His global vision and ability to mobilize people through speeches show Gemini's persuasive side, though his methods and outcomes remain polarizing.

**Aung San Suu Kyi (Born June 19, 1945)**: A Burmese political figure who campaigned for democracy in Myanmar, receiving international recognition.

**Gemini Traits**: Composed numerous speeches and letters that rallied supporters globally. She navigated complex political terrain, reflecting adaptability, though her later tenure in power brought controversy.

These examples demonstrate that Gemini expressions are not confined to a single region or style. Whether pushing political reform or leading social movements, the sign's energy can manifest as a desire to communicate visions of change. Yet, again, the complexities of each historical context exceed simple zodiac explanations.

## Misconceptions About Fame and Signs

Some fans might believe that being a Gemini automatically means one is destined for fame. That is not accurate. Every sign can find renown, depending on personal dedication, environment, and luck. The achievements of famous Geminis simply highlight that when natural Gemini attributes—like flexible thinking and communication—merge with effort, opportunities can arise.

**Destiny vs. Choice**: These famous individuals likely put in years of practice, overcame setbacks, and harnessed their distinct personalities productively.

**The Quiet Geminis**: Many Geminis excel in fields that do not attract big headlines—like teaching, community leadership, small business, or family roles—yet their qualities can still shine.

**No Guarantee of Success**: Talent alone does not ensure prominence. Timing, market conditions, and personal networks also matter.

So, while reading about accomplished Geminis, it is best to view their zodiac sign as one piece of the puzzle rather than a sole reason for their success.

## Celebrity Culture and Gemini

In modern celebrity culture, the interest in Gemini public figures might stem from the sign's ability to surprise audiences. Fans tune in, curious to see if a Gemini icon will change direction musically, politically, or aesthetically. This unpredictability can keep the media fascinated.

**Headlines**: Geminis can make headlines by announcing sudden new ventures, stirring debates on social media, or unveiling a fresh personal style.

**Keeping Relevance**: Some celebrities shift from movies to TV, from singing to hosting, or from performing to activism. This resembles the Gemini pattern of exploring uncharted territory.

Yet, the media might also criticize them for being "all over the place," ignoring how methodical they can be behind the scenes. Celebrity watchers should remember that public images are just that—images. The real person may be more focused and thoughtful than gossip headlines imply.

## Intersection with Other Birth Chart Elements

Famous Geminis also have other zodiac elements in their natal charts. For instance, a Gemini with a grounded earth sign moon might approach projects more steadily, or a fiery rising sign might intensify their outward persona. Although we often talk about the sun sign, deeper astrological context helps explain personality nuances.

**Example**: An actor with a Gemini sun, Scorpio moon, and Leo rising might blend quick mental leaps with intense emotional presence and a flashy public approach. This could yield an especially dynamic stage performance.

**Public Interpretations**: Fans who see only the Gemini side might be surprised by behind-the-scenes seriousness or strong loyalty. Each chart dimension colors how a person expresses or manages Gemini qualities.

Without full charts, we see only glimpses of these complexities. Still, the common Gemini thread often remains: fluid communication, interest in novelty, and a diverse approach to careers.

## Timing and Shifts in Popularity

Many public figures have highs and lows in popularity. A Gemini's ability to reinvent themselves can help them climb back after a lull, or pivot to a new avenue if one path closes. This capacity to rebrand or tackle a fresh domain might account for the longevity of certain Gemini careers.

**Examples of Reinvention:**

**Musical Shifts**: A singer who jumps from one genre to a very different style, surprising fans.

**Political Repositioning**: A leader who changes platforms or alliances to match evolving voter concerns.

**Personal Branding**: Actors who shift from comedic roles to dramatic ones, proving their range and staying relevant.

In each scenario, the risk is losing older fans, but Geminis may gain new ones drawn by the novelty. The capacity to rebound from setbacks via a new approach can be a hallmark of those with strong Gemini influences.

## Gemini Pioneers in New Media

With technology opening new platforms—like YouTube, podcasting, or social media content—modern Geminis can harness digital communication to reach audiences quickly. Some become internet stars by posting vlogs, comedic sketches, or commentary, thriving on the quick turnaround of viewer feedback.

**Traits That Excel in New Media:**

**Rapid Content Creation**: Geminis can whip up ideas, record them, edit, and upload swiftly.

**Direct Interaction**: Real-time comments, live chats, or Q&A sessions feed into Gemini's love of two-way communication.

**Adaptation**: If a trend changes or a platform introduces new features, Geminis can pivot fast.

Viewers who appreciate lively dialogue or frequent content updates may gravitate toward creators with a Gemini style. But, as with all success, consistency and genuine engagement matter just as much as star signs.

## Reflecting on Failures and Growth

Some Geminis soared high, then fell from grace through scandal or personal struggles. Observing how they handle failure can show the sign's resilience. In adversity, they might rely on strong communication to defend themselves or attempt to change public perception. That does not always succeed, but it demonstrates the Gemini impulse to solve problems through discussion or by reworking their public image.

**Path to Redemption**: If a Gemini figure publicly apologizes, clarifies, and changes direction, fans might see it as a "classic Gemini pivot." But the sincerity behind it is shaped by personal integrity, not just star sign traits.

**Learning from Mistakes**: Many share personal lessons in interviews or books, bridging their experiences with broader audiences. The sign's ability to articulate new understandings can help them connect again after controversies.

It underscores that fame alone does not guarantee wisdom or moral standing. Each person's internal moral compass shapes their responses to mistakes.

## Cultural Differences in Recognition

How Geminis are recognized can depend heavily on cultural views of fame. In some regions, a gifted mathematician or philosopher might achieve a level of respect akin to celebrity status, while in others, sporting heroes or film stars dominate the concept of "famous." Therefore, certain Gemini talents might shine more in societies that value intellectual discourse, while others flourish in entertainment-driven cultures.

**Western Celebrity vs. Local Icons**: A Gemini poet revered in one country might be unknown elsewhere if global media does not highlight them.

**Language Barriers**: If a Gemini's main output is in a less international language, it may limit global recognition, even if their work is groundbreaking locally.

Consequently, our list of well-known Gemini figures often leans Western or mainstream. There are certainly numerous Gemini luminaries in smaller or non-English-speaking contexts, overshadowed by global media focus.

## Timeless vs. Trend-Driven

Some Geminis remain timeless icons because their adaptability reflects universal human experiences—like exploring new boundaries or bridging different viewpoints. Others might fade if their fame relies solely on short-lived trends or social media hype. The difference often lies in how they handle transitions:

**Longevity**: Figures who continuously refine their craft or reinvent themselves with substance remain relevant across generations.

**Trend Burnout**: If it is purely about novelty, fans might move on once the excitement dulls, and the individual never expands beyond that initial interest.

Geminis can harness their flexible nature to evolve in meaningful ways, rather than chasing novelty for novelty's sake.

## Looking Ahead: Future Gemini Leaders and Creators

As the world keeps changing, emerging Gemini talents might find new platforms to express themselves—virtual reality, interactive story gaming, or advanced research fields. They will likely bring the same core traits:

**Experimental Approaches**: Trying untested methods or bridging multiple disciplines.

**Communicative Leadership**: Using digital tools to engage broad audiences.

**Restless Ideas**: Pushing boundaries of what is possible in art, science, or social movements.

We can anticipate future Gemini figures will keep surprising the public, forming communities around their dynamic messages, or forging revolutions in how we share knowledge.

# CHAPTER 19: GEMINI THROUGH DIFFERENT AGES

Geminis are known for their active minds, talkative nature, and eagerness to learn new things. However, the way these traits appear can vary depending on what stage of life they are in. A Gemini child might display curiosity by asking endless questions, while a Gemini teenager may enjoy trying many different clubs and sports. An older Gemini might take up new hobbies or continue exploring fresh ideas even after retirement. In this chapter, we will look at how Gemini qualities might show themselves as a person grows older. We will avoid repeating earlier content in detail, focusing instead on the unique ways Geminis adapt and thrive at each life stage.

## Gemini in Early Childhood

When Geminis are very young (ages 1 to 5), they are often bright-eyed and inquisitive. They might point at everything around them, wanting to know names or how things work. Even before they speak full sentences, they can be chatty in their own way, babbling or testing sounds to see how people respond.

**Curiosity**: A Gemini toddler may love exploring. They might crawl toward every cupboard or stack of toys, wanting to discover new objects. This can lead to a lot of "Why?" questions as soon as they can talk.

**Early Speech**: Many Geminis show an interest in speaking sooner than some peers. They might pick up words quickly or mimic phrases. They enjoy short, lively exchanges with adults.

**Playful Learning**: Because of their busy minds, they might enjoy educational toys that make sounds or allow them to press buttons. They also love stories that feature imaginative plots.

**Challenges for Parents**

**Keeping Up**: Parents might find it tricky to satisfy all of a Gemini toddler's questions and explorations. It is important to guide them gently without stifling their eagerness.

**Short Attention Span**: A Gemini child might jump from one toy to another. Offering a mix of short, engaging activities can suit them better than expecting them to stick with one toy for hours.

At this stage, Geminis benefit from warm encouragement to ask questions, as well as simple answers that do not overwhelm them. Playing word games or naming objects during daily routines can feed their young minds in a relaxed, age-appropriate way.

## Gemini in Later Childhood

As Geminis move into later childhood (ages 6 to 10), their love for conversation and variety often intensifies. They could be the ones in class raising their hands first, or reading about random topics at home. School becomes a fun place for them to gather facts and share with friends.

**Love of Reading**: Many Gemini kids discover they love books—particularly if those books cover interesting facts, quirky stories, or a bit of humor. They might also enjoy short chapter books they can discuss with classmates.

**Storytelling**: Writing or telling small tales can be appealing. Gemini children might invent characters or read stories aloud to the family.

**Group Play**: They often enjoy playing in groups because it involves sharing ideas, talking, and inventing new games on the spot.

**Potential Struggles**

**Sitting Still**: If lessons are repetitive, a Gemini child might become restless. Parents and teachers can introduce variety in learning.

**Classroom Distractions**: They might chat with friends or daydream about new topics when bored. Structured activities that keep them challenged can help.

By this age, encouraging them to join clubs or groups that let them practice social and mental skills—like a book club, puzzle club, or something creative—can keep them engaged. It also helps them learn how to listen to others and wait for their turn, balancing their natural urge to talk.

## Gemini in Pre-Teen and Early Teens

Around ages 11 to 14, Geminis enter a phase where social circles and personal identity become more important. They might explore new friend groups, bounce between different interests, and test out varied styles or activities. This can be an exciting but sometimes confusing period.

**Searching for Hobbies**: A Gemini might sign up for drama club, then switch to a robotics team, and then consider trying a sport. They want to explore many areas before focusing on any single one.

**Expanding Friendships**: They might have friends from different groups—some who like sports, others who like art—because Geminis find something interesting in each. This can give them a wide social circle, though they might not be super close to every friend.

**Emerging Sense of Self**: They look for ways to express their thoughts. If they have access to social media (depending on parental rules), they might share jokes, videos, or short blogs. It is a way to connect with people and show some of their varied ideas.

### Challenges

**Peer Pressure**: Because Geminis adapt easily, they might feel pulled into multiple friend circles with different expectations. They could lose track of their own preferences if they try too hard to fit in everywhere.

**Inconsistent Motivation**: They might start a big school project eagerly but want to jump to another one halfway through. Gentle reminders and small deadlines help them finish tasks on time.

At this age, parents or mentors can guide them by pointing out their strengths—perhaps praising their good communication or problem-solving—while teaching them about setting realistic goals. It is also helpful to provide private spaces for them to reflect, as they can be talkative but also need quiet moments to process all these new experiences.

## Gemini in Later Teens

From about 15 to 18, a Gemini's personality might become more defined, yet they still experiment. They may take advanced classes or pick extracurriculars that let them explore academic or creative interests. Socially, they might shift friend circles if they outgrow certain dynamics. Romantic interests can also appear, leading to the possibility of first real relationships.

**Intellectual Interests**: A Gemini teen may lean toward debate clubs, student government, or writing for the school newspaper. It fits their desire to share opinions and gather information.

**Social Complexity**: They might juggle multiple friend groups, from sports teammates to bandmates. This broad involvement can be fun but might be time-consuming.

**Romantic Curiosity**: They might show interest in relationships, enjoying the flirtation stage and the mental back-and-forth that romance can bring. They want a partner who can keep up with their jokes and share interesting conversations.

### Potential Struggles

**Future Plans**: They might feel uncertain about picking a career path or college major, since many topics appeal to them. Sorting out a single route can be overwhelming.

**Emotional Depth**: They could face heartbreak or conflict if they date, especially if they misread a partner's needs or switch interests too fast. Learning to show consistent care is key.

This stage can be an exciting period for a Gemini teen to develop leadership skills and deeper emotional intelligence. They can also learn how to handle bigger responsibilities—like part-time jobs or significant academic projects—teaching them to balance spontaneity with steadiness.

## Gemini in Early Adulthood

In early adulthood (roughly ages 19 to 29), Geminis might explore new freedoms: living away from family, pursuing higher education or job opportunities, and forging adult relationships. Their Gemini traits often shine in networking, job interviews, or social events.

**College or Workforce Exploration**: They may switch majors or job roles if they feel they have not found their passion. This is a normal part of finding what truly excites them.

**New Friendships and Partnerships**: A Gemini may connect with colleagues or friends from different backgrounds, enjoying the variety. If they date, they might still test different relationship styles before committing.

**Multi-Tasking**: Their calendar could fill up with professional tasks, social outings, creative side projects, and more. They thrive on the bustle but risk burnout if not careful.

### Challenges

**Career Focus**: Some Geminis might be labeled as "job-hoppers." Potential employers might question their steadiness. With self-awareness, they can show that each new job or role is a step in broadening skills, not a sign of flakiness.

**Financial Management**: A Gemini could be tempted to overspend on gadgets, travel, or classes that promise excitement. Learning budgeting can be vital here.

Early adulthood is a time to sharpen time-management skills and figure out personal goals. Geminis who find ways to turn their wide interests into a cohesive direction—like a multi-faceted career path—often flourish.

## Gemini in Their 30s and 40s

By the time Geminis reach their 30s and 40s, many have gathered a range of experiences. Some settle into stable careers that offer enough mental variety—like marketing, teaching, or technology—while others prefer freelancing or entrepreneurship to keep options open. Family life may also become a bigger theme, whether raising children or caring for relatives.

**Career Growth**: They might climb career ladders if the job keeps them mentally engaged. Others start their own businesses, merging different skill sets.

**Community Involvement**: With more life experience, Geminis might join local clubs, speak at events, or organize get-togethers. They use their communication to bring people together.

**Parenting Style**: If they have children, Geminis often encourage them to explore multiple hobbies and ask questions. They can be playful parents, though they must provide routines and stability children need.

**Potential Pitfalls**

**Midlife Doubts**: If they feel stuck in a repetitive role, a Gemini might long for change. This could lead to mid-career shifts or "side hustles" to reignite passion.

**Over-Commitment**: Between work, family, and personal interests, they might spread themselves too thin. Learning to prioritize is crucial.

This stage can be quite fulfilling if a Gemini combines their curiosity with the wisdom gained from earlier mistakes. They might become mentors themselves, guiding younger folks with a lively teaching style.

# Gemini in Their 50s and 60s

Around 50 to 60, a Gemini may reach a point of established expertise or leadership roles, while still looking for fresh challenges. If they have grown comfortable in a certain field, they might become known for quick thinking, problem-solving, or team-building. Alternatively, they might leap into an entirely new interest.

**Career Mastery**: They can use decades of experience to handle complex tasks elegantly, relying on wide knowledge. Some might shift to consulting or leading workshops.

**Empty Nest or Changing Home Life**: If children have grown up, a Gemini might enjoy newfound freedom to travel, start side projects, or pick up old hobbies.

**Community Respect**: They might have a reputation as a lively speaker or organizer, frequently asked to give talks or moderate discussions. Others turn to them for advice.

### Challenges

**Health and Stress**: With high activity levels, stress might take a toll unless they find time for rest or gentle exercise.

**Balancing Identity**: They have tried many roles by now—so they should confirm what truly makes them happy, rather than chasing every new possibility.

During the 50s and 60s, Geminis who maintain an open mind can keep life interesting and meaningful. They might volunteer or help local groups, using their communication skills for good causes.

# Gemini in Retirement or Later Years (70+)

Geminis in their 70s or beyond might show that age does not stop curiosity. Whether it is technology, gardening, or reading about world events, they continue to feed their minds. Social connections can remain important—some might mentor younger folks, join clubs, or simply chat with neighbors.

**Continued Learning**: They may join senior classes or discussion groups to keep their mental spark alive. They might read widely—magazines, online articles, or even sign up for small local courses.

**Storytelling**: A Gemini elder might share life stories or wisdom with grandchildren or community members, offering witty or insightful narratives.

**Adaptive Lifestyles**: If physical mobility changes, they adjust by exploring accessible activities—like online chess, writing memoirs, or video-calling distant relatives.

**Potential Pitfalls**

**Loneliness**: If their social circle shrinks, they could feel restless. Seeking out community meetups or volunteer roles can help.

**Health Issues**: Geminis might need to moderate their busy approach, focusing on gentle routines that keep them active but not overextended.

In older age, Geminis can remain shining examples of lifelong learners. They may surprise family members by picking up new skills or hosting gatherings. Their spirit can stay agile, reminding everyone that curiosity does not have an expiration date.

## Across All Ages: Themes That Stay

No matter the stage—childhood, teenage years, adulthood, or older age—some Gemini patterns stay consistent:

**Desire to Communicate**: They enjoy talking, writing, or otherwise sharing thoughts. The exact form might shift from crayons to typed emails, but the basic impulse remains.

**Flexibility**: Geminis handle changes relatively well, be it switching hobbies or adapting to new life circumstances. They value novelty and movement.

**Curiosity**: They continually ask questions, read, or investigate. Even seniors might experiment with new tech devices or local community events.

**Potential Restlessness**: They can become bored or edgy if stuck in repetitive situations. They need mental variety to stay motivated.

Understanding these themes can help Geminis or their loved ones provide supportive environments. Each life stage can benefit from a mix of structure (to ensure they finish tasks or remain grounded) and freedom (to explore multiple avenues).

## Guidance for Parents of Young Geminis

For parents or guardians raising a Gemini child, certain approaches might help them flourish:

**Answer Questions Patiently**: When they ask "Why?" or "How?" repeatedly, try to respond calmly or suggest ways to find answers together.

**Encourage Variety**: Offer different types of books, experiences, or family outings to keep their curiosity satisfied.

**Set Gentle Boundaries**: If they bounce from one activity to another, guide them to complete at least one small project before switching, teaching them perseverance.

**Teach Empathy**: Even though they love words, help them understand when to pause and listen deeply. Role-playing or talking about feelings can build emotional awareness.

By blending these steps with consistent warmth and acceptance of their talkative nature, you can help them develop confidence in exploring the world.

## Tips for Teen Geminis' Growth

During teen years, Geminis benefit from certain life skills that expand beyond basic talk.

**Time Management**: They might keep a planner or phone reminders, so they do not forget assignments or double-book social events.

**Healthy Expression of Feelings**: Encourage them to write a journal or talk about deeper emotions rather than only focusing on outward chatter.

**Choosing Activities**: They might want to join every club. Suggest focusing on two or three they truly love, to avoid burnout.

Teens who learn these lessons often carry them into adulthood with more poise, lessening the risk of conflicts or regrets.

## Supporting Geminis in Their 20s and 30s

This is a time for career development, personal relationships, and big decisions. Friends or partners can help Geminis by:

**Offering Guidance, Not Control**: Instead of telling them they are "too scattered," help them see patterns in their interests. They might find a career that uses multiple talents.

**Being Willing to Experiment**: If they want to travel or try an unconventional path, hearing supportive feedback can encourage them while still offering practical advice about finances or planning.

**Reminding Them to Rest**: A Gemini might run from event to event. Gentle suggestions to slow down or schedule relaxation can prevent stress.

When handled with understanding, these decades can yield a rich tapestry of experiences, with Geminis fine-tuning their sense of purpose.

## Guidance for Geminis in Their 40s and 50s

Sometimes midlife can spark changes or a sense of reevaluation. Geminis might question whether their job or lifestyle still satisfies their curiosity.

**Reassessing Goals**: They could list what still excites them and what feels draining. A shift in career or hobbies may reinvigorate their spirit.

**Building on Expertise**: By now, they have a lot of knowledge to share. Creating workshops, writing articles, or mentoring younger folks can unify their experiences.

**Strengthening Important Bonds**: They might focus on family or close friends, ensuring they invest enough time in deeper emotional connections rather than always meeting new acquaintances.

Showing that growth never ends, they can keep exploring but with a steadier wisdom.

## Enjoying Later Life for Geminis

For Geminis in older age, staying mentally active is vital. They might read daily, do puzzles, or join discussion groups. If health allows, short trips or new classes can fuel their mind. The main idea is to keep variety alive but not overstress themselves physically.

**Grandparent Role**: Telling stories to grandkids, playing word or number games, and encouraging curiosity in younger generations can be fulfilling.

**Reflecting on Life**: Some Geminis write memoirs or blog about their experiences, weaving humorous or thoughtful observations. They might host small gatherings to share memories and advice.

**Tech Engagement**: Many older Geminis enjoy learning new gadgets or social media to stay connected with family. This can keep them feeling part of modern life.

Even if the body slows, the Gemini mind can remain bright and open, turning advanced age into a stage of gentle discovery.

## Across the Generations: Gemini Family Traits

If multiple family members are Geminis, or if a younger Gemini has an older relative with the same sign, they might compare notes. It can be fun to see how two Geminis handle day-to-day life differently. Perhaps an older

Gemini has learned to manage restlessness, while a younger one is still figuring it out. In the process, they can share tips like:

**Handling Stress**: The older one might recall times they took on too many tasks, explaining how they overcame burnout.

**Communicating Calmly**: They might demonstrate how to avoid interrupting or how to hold back when the other person is emotional.

**Choosing Directions Wisely**: They might highlight how focusing on a core interest led to deeper success, rather than scattering efforts.

Such cross-generational chats can lead to strong bonds and mutual learning.

## Healthy Progress at Every Age

As Geminis progress, each milestone offers a chance to refine their communication, explore new areas, and expand emotional depth. Maintaining balanced growth often involves:

**Embracing Mistakes**: In childhood or older adulthood, Geminis might leap into an idea that does not work out. Accepting that as part of learning helps them avoid negative self-talk.

**Emotional Awareness**: While mental interests remain, paying attention to feelings and building empathy is a lifelong journey.

**Continuing Curiosity**: Even in stable routines, they can find mini-adventures—like reading a new genre, visiting local exhibitions, or attending short workshops.

Regardless of age, a Gemini's spark can shine if they keep an open mind and a caring heart.

## Unique Career Turns

Some Geminis shift careers at ages 40, 50, or even 60. For example, a middle-aged Gemini who was a teacher might decide to write children's books, leveraging communication and imagination. Another could retire from corporate life and become a travel blogger, tapping into their love for variety. These late changes can boost morale, making them feel rejuvenated.

**Managing Risks**: Each shift can carry financial or emotional risks. Geminis must weigh the pros and cons carefully, and perhaps get guidance from family or professionals.

**Linking Past Skills**: Even a brand-new career can use old experiences. Geminis can unify these experiences in unexpected ways. For instance, if they were once a sales manager, they can apply marketing and people skills to writing or counseling.

Such career pivots show that a Gemini's thirst for newness does not vanish—it simply adapts to life's circumstances.

## Emotional Growth Over Time

When young, Geminis might handle disputes with quick words or by changing their focus. As they mature, they often see the value of slowing down, acknowledging deeper feelings, and working through conflicts carefully. This emotional growth can enhance their relationships at any age—friendships, romances, or family ties.

**Realizing Depth**: They may come to understand that not every situation can be fixed with a clever phrase. Sometimes they must sit with uncomfortable feelings, or let someone else vent.

**Improving Listening**: Over the decades, Geminis might become more skilled at giving space for others' stories. This fosters trust and shows that they are truly present, not just waiting to speak.

**Balancing Head and Heart**: They could integrate logic with genuine empathy. If someone is sad, they apply reason and compassion. For them, it is not about ignoring reason but merging it with real emotional support.

By the time they are older, many Geminis display a calmer approach. They still enjoy a good talk, but they also appreciate quiet times when closeness does not need a thousand words.

## Spiritual and Philosophical Growth

Some Geminis use their curiosity to explore spiritual or philosophical questions in midlife or later. They might read about different faiths, attend diverse seminars, or talk with many people about life's big mysteries. This can enrich their sense of meaning.

**Exploring Many Views**: They do not just settle on one perspective quickly. They may sample a variety of teachings.

**Asking Deeper Questions**: Their innate "Why?" extends to existence, purpose, and ethics. They might keep journals of insights or discuss them in group gatherings.

**Mixing Practical Logic**: Even if they embrace a spiritual path, Geminis often keep a logical side, analyzing how rituals or beliefs function. They might combine heartfelt devotion with reasoning.

This philosophical searching can become another layer of mental stimulation. Some might find a stable system that speaks to them, others stay in a broad exploration, and either path can bring satisfaction if approached sincerely.

# CHAPTER 20: UNDERSTANDING GEMINI BETTER

We have examined countless aspects of the Gemini sign: from basic qualities like quick thinking and a love for variety, to how Geminis interact in friendships, family, school, work, and beyond. We have explored famous Geminis who demonstrated communication skills, adaptability, and a willingness to shift paths. We have also seen how Geminis grow through different life stages, maintaining a bright, curious spirit while adapting to each phase.

Now, let us bring these insights together, offering a final look at what it means to understand Gemini at a deeper level. This closing chapter underscores the key factors that shape a Gemini's path, the myths that can cloud their true character, and practical tips for both Geminis and those around them. By the end, we will have a well-rounded view of this multifaceted sign, able to appreciate Gemini's uniqueness while supporting their need for change and mental spark.

## Core Traits Revisited

A large part of "understanding Gemini better" is recognizing the fundamental characteristics that show up over and over in their lives:

**Curiosity**: Geminis are drawn to new facts, experiences, and people. This leads them to ask questions, attend various events, or read about diverse subjects.

**Strong Communication**: Talking, writing, texting—Geminis thrive on expressing themselves. They enjoy friendly debates, comedic chats, or serious discussions that let them share ideas.

**Quick Thinking**: Their mental agility helps them connect dots fast, see multiple angles, or come up with witty remarks. This can make them excellent problem-solvers, debaters, or organizers.

**Love of Variety**: They switch activities or try new hobbies regularly. They might have a broad social circle spanning different interests.

**Adaptability**: When faced with changing circumstances, Geminis can handle sudden shifts well, using flexibility to find new solutions.

Any close understanding of Gemini involves these traits as a baseline, whether we are talking about them as children, workers, partners, or seniors.

## Factors That Shape a Gemini's Path

It is also important to see that each Gemini's life story depends on more than star sign traits. Key elements include:

**Environment**: A supportive family or teacher can channel their curiosity positively, while a limiting environment might frustrate them.

**Choices**: Over time, Geminis make decisions—like focusing on a particular field or sticking with a stable job—if it aligns with their deeper goals, despite their love for variety.

**Other Astrological Influences**: Moon signs, rising signs, and planetary positions can change how a Gemini's basic qualities manifest. For instance, a Gemini with a water sign moon might be more emotionally open.

**Personal Growth**: They learn from mistakes. A younger Gemini might talk over people, but an older Gemini may have sharpened listening skills.

Hence, although we see general patterns, it is wise to keep each person's unique blend of experiences and personality traits in mind.

## Recognizing a Balanced Gemini

A Gemini who has found healthy ways to live out their sign's potential often shows balance:

**Curiosity with Follow-Through**: They still explore multiple topics but have learned to complete tasks or maintain important commitments.

**Communication with Listening**: They speak up but also pause to hear others' views. They know when to be quiet or let someone vent.

**Adaptability without Chaos**: They can pivot or switch approaches in a plan but do so thoughtfully, communicating changes to others.

**Social Involvement with Boundaries**: They have broad networks but recognize the value of deeper relationships. They do not overextend themselves in 20 different groups at once.

When a Gemini reaches this balanced state, they can excel in personal and professional realms, making use of their talents without being seen as unreliable or scattered.

## Pitfalls That Can Block Growth

Geminis are not immune to falling into traps that hinder their progress or strain relationships. Some pitfalls include:

**Information Overload**: Taking on too many facts or tasks can lead to confusion or incomplete work.

**Gossip or Surface Talk**: If they never delve into deeper topics, they can remain stuck in shallow conversation cycles, failing to build genuine connections.

**Overreaction to Boredom**: Feeling bored does not always mean it is time to abandon a project. Sometimes, pushing through a lull leads to deeper rewards.

**Miscommunication**: Their fast speech can spark misunderstandings, especially if they jump to conclusions or do not clarify their intent.

A Gemini who becomes aware of these pitfalls can work on them, often by setting small goals, practicing patience in conversations, or using planning tools to organize multiple interests.

## Overcoming Myths

Earlier chapters discussed myths like "Geminis are two-faced," "Geminis cannot commit," or "Geminis only care about talking." Overcoming these misconceptions involves:

**Self-Awareness**: Geminis who openly acknowledge they can appear inconsistent help others see the difference between open-mindedness and dishonesty.

**Proving Reliability**: By meeting deadlines, being on time for social events, and finishing tasks, Geminis can show they are not flaky, even if they love variety.

**Explaining Communication Style**: Letting friends or partners know that switching topics does not mean ignoring them, but rather a natural mental shift, can ease tensions.

Myths will persist, but consistent actions and respectful communication can prove them wrong in daily life.

## Gemini Strengths in Different Life Areas

We can briefly outline how Gemini's strengths can shine if applied well:

**School and Learning**: Quick grasp of concepts, enjoyment of group projects, and lively class participation. If they focus, they can become star students, especially in language or social subjects.

**Work and Careers**: Agile thinking suits fields like journalism, marketing, teaching, sales, tech start-ups, or anything requiring adaptability. They often do well in roles that let them interact with coworkers or clients.

**Family and Parenting**: Bringing humor and knowledge to the household, encouraging children or siblings to stay curious, planning fun family activities, and being open to new experiences.

**Friendships**: Offering variety, introducing group members to new ideas, helping to coordinate plans, and resolving conflicts through open dialogue.

**Romantic Relationships**: Keeping the partnership fresh with date ideas, thoughtful talks, or joint adventures. However, they must also build trust through consistency and emotional sharing.

Balancing each area with genuine follow-through and empathy can lead to a fulfilling life.

## Advice for Geminis Who Feel Stuck

Sometimes a Gemini feels trapped if they are in a dull routine or face demands that leave no room for exploration. If that happens:

**Add Small Sparks**: Insert variety in small ways, like reading new books on a break or rearranging a workspace. Even minor changes can lift their mood.

**Seek Mentors**: Talking to more experienced people can inspire them to find a route that blends novelty with structure.

**Try a Short Course**: If they cannot make a big career change, a few weeks in a side course or hobby might re-energize them.

**Reassess Goals**: They can ask, "Am I bored because I have outgrown this path, or do I just need a new challenge within the same environment?"

A Gemini does not always have to leap from one big change to another. Sometimes subtle shifts are enough to refresh their sense of possibility.

## Tips for Loved Ones Interacting with Geminis

People who share homes or daily contact with Geminis can find ways to deepen harmony:

**Embrace Conversation**: Show interest when a Gemini talks about random subjects. Offer your thoughts or follow-up questions. This builds mutual respect.

**Set Boundaries Kindly**: If you need quiet time, explain it nicely, so the Gemini knows you are not rejecting them. Geminis can respect alone time if it is communicated without anger.

**Suggest Joint Adventures**: Let them propose ideas, or surprise them with a novel outing. They will likely appreciate the spontaneity.

**Maintain Direct Honesty**: Geminis value honest feedback. If something bothers you, share it calmly rather than letting it fester.

Relationships often grow stronger when loved ones realize that Gemini's constant mental movement is not flightiness but enthusiasm for life.

## Planning Tools for the Busy Gemini

Because Geminis can juggle many tasks, certain tools or habits help them manage:

**Digital or Paper Planners**: A flexible layout that allows them to list tasks, but also add quick notes, might suit them.

**Color Coding**: Marking different activities or deadlines in bright colors can help them see everything clearly at a glance.

**Short Task Blocks**: Breaking a large task into small, timed segments (like 25-minute focus periods, followed by short breaks) fits their attention style.

**Morning Checklists**: Starting the day by reviewing a short list can keep them on track, preventing random distractions.

These methods let Geminis keep their varied schedule under control while still leaving room for spontaneity.

## Emotional Support for Gemini's Sensitive Side

Even though Geminis may appear confident or chatty, they sometimes need emotional reassurance:

**Listen Attentively**: Let them voice worries or regrets without jumping in.

**Validate Feelings**: Acknowledge their struggles are real, even if they express them in a logical or joking tone.

**Encourage Reflection**: Journaling or talking in depth about emotions can help them see patterns.

**Offer Solitude**: While they love talking, they also might need quiet time if their mind feels overloaded. Suggest a walk or a restful break.

Balancing outward talk with inward reflection helps Geminis handle stress or sadness more smoothly.

## Healthy Routines for Gemini Well-Being

Physical and mental well-being is crucial for any sign, and Geminis sometimes overlook rest or consistent exercise because they chase new interests. A few practical tips:

**Short, Fun Workouts**: Activities like dancing, group classes, or sports with friends keep them engaged better than repetitive routines.

**Balanced Eating**: With their busy schedules, Geminis might skip meals or grab fast snacks. They can benefit from planning simple, healthy options.

**Mindful Downtime**: At least once a day, Geminis can pause phone notifications or step away from social media for mental clarity.

**Sleep Habits**: Setting a bedtime can help them avoid staying up too late reading or chatting online.

By weaving these routines into daily life, Geminis maintain enough energy to explore the things they love without burning out.

## Work Strategies for Professional Success

In professional contexts, Geminis can stand out if they use their strengths wisely:

**Team Collaboration**: They often make good project coordinators or communication leads, bridging ideas between team members.

**Public Speaking or Presentations**: If a workplace needs someone to present proposals, Geminis can make it interesting and clear.

**Avoid Overcommitment**: The risk is signing up for multiple tasks. Learning to say "no" or seeking help on less urgent tasks can ensure they deliver high-quality results.

**Networking**: Their easygoing approach to conversation helps them form valuable professional connections. However, they should maintain those relationships with genuine follow-up, not just initial excitement.

With a bit of structure, Geminis can turn their mental agility into tangible career progress and respect from colleagues.

## Strengthening Close Bonds

We have covered relationships in detail, but here are final pointers for Geminis to maintain healthy bonds with friends, partners, or family:

**Schedule One-on-One Time**: Even a simple coffee meet-up or video call to talk without distractions can nourish deeper connections.

**Remember Special Dates**: Setting reminders for birthdays, anniversaries, or key events helps them show they value others.

**Apologize When Needed**: If they forgot an appointment or said something too bluntly, a sincere apology can mend fences.

**Show Consistency**: Doing small consistent acts, like checking in daily or keeping certain routines, can reassure loved ones that the relationship is secure.

Over time, these practices can reduce misunderstandings that arise from the "Gemini is unpredictable" myth.

## Gemini's Creative Outlets

One way Geminis stay balanced is channeling their mental flow into creative pursuits. This might include:

**Writing**: Short stories, poetry, or blogging about their day.

**Art or Design**: Experimenting with painting, digital art, or crafts. They may not stick to one medium forever but can produce interesting pieces along the way.

**Performance**: Stand-up comedy, open mic nights, or even giving fun presentations can let them amuse or enlighten audiences.

Such outlets give them a sense of fulfillment, let them connect with others, and keep that restless mind happily occupied.

## Travel and Discovery

Exploring new places can be a highlight for Geminis, whether it is day trips, bigger vacations, or virtual tours. They enjoy visiting museums, historical sites, or unique local spots to gather stories and experiences.

**Short Escapes**: Even a weekend trip to a nearby town can spark excitement.

**Long Journeys**: Some Geminis try backpacking or multi-country tours, meeting different cultures.

**Cultural Exchanges**: They might take language courses abroad or stay with local hosts, satisfying their curiosity about everyday life in other regions.

Travel not only expands their knowledge but can feed their social side if they interact with locals or fellow travelers.

## Handling Anxiety and Overthinking

A Gemini's mind can race, sometimes resulting in anxiety if they overthink problems or fear missing out on better options. Tools to cope include:

**Breathing Techniques**: Focusing on slow, steady breaths for a few moments can calm a swirling mind.

**Grounding Exercises**: Naming five things they see or hear around them helps bring them back to the present moment.

**Talking with a Counselor or Trusted Friend**: Verbalizing worries can help them see solutions.

**Realistic Goal-Setting**: Breaking big tasks or decisions into smaller steps reduces feeling overwhelmed.

These methods let Geminis harness their active thoughts instead of being controlled by them.

## Emotional Intelligence and Maturity

As Geminis mature, combining logic with emotional depth becomes a real strength:

**Reading Social Cues**: Noticing how body language or tone of voice changes helps them respond better, rather than continuing their own monologue.

**Empathy Development**: Understanding that some people need more reassurance, or that certain topics might be sensitive, leads to kinder conversations.

**Reflective Dialogue**: Instead of only delivering quick remarks, they can slow down and say, "It sounds like you are upset because of this reason—am I right?" This fosters real understanding.

Geminis who cultivate emotional intelligence can become leaders who inspire trust, or friends who offer genuine support.

## Encouraging Children to Understand Gemini

If a child is born a Gemini or shows Gemini traits, teaching them about these qualities can empower them. They might appreciate hearing that their "many questions" and "chatty style" are strengths. Of course, we must guide them to also:

**Stay Patient**: Not all tasks are instantly fun, but finishing them can lead to bigger rewards.

**Stay Humble**: Quick thinking is great, but listening to slower or quieter people might reveal valuable insights they would otherwise miss.

By learning self-awareness early, the child can avoid frustrations or negative labels.

## Looking Forward: The Future for Geminis

In a rapidly changing world—where technology, social norms, and job markets shift—Geminis' adaptability can be a true advantage. They might:

**Embrace Digital Platforms**: Flourish as online content creators, educators, or community builders.

**Lead in Innovation**: Try new tools or business ideas while others hesitate.

**Bridge Gaps**: Bring together different groups, using communication to unify people around common goals.

As the future demands flexible thinking and quick learning, Geminis are well-positioned to shine when they focus their energies effectively.

# Final Thoughts: Embracing Gemini's Potential

The Gemini sign represents a lively spirit that can bring wonder to daily life, push boundaries, and foster connections. Yet, it also calls for self-control to avoid scattering energy too thinly. By blending curiosity with steadiness, Geminis can become powerful voices in their communities, families, and workplaces. They can remain lifelong learners who share knowledge generously, adapt to changes with grace, and handle relationships with sincerity.

Whether you are a Gemini yourself, have a Gemini in your family, or befriend one, understanding these core traits and how they evolve over time can lead to better support and companionship. A Gemini who feels accepted for their thirst for variety—while gently guided to keep commitments—often grows into a confident, creative, and compassionate person. Their wit and broad interests can enrich many lives, proving that a free mind, when balanced with care, is a treasure to everyone around.

# Help Us Share Your Thoughts!

**Dear reader,**

Thank you for spending your time with this book. We hope it brought you enjoyment and a few new ideas to think about. If there was anything that didn't work for you, or if you have suggestions on how we can improve, please let us know at **kontakt@skriuwer.com**. Your feedback means a lot to us and helps us make our books even better.

If you enjoyed this book, we would be very grateful if you left a review on the site where you purchased it. Your review not only helps other readers find our books, but also encourages us to keep creating more stories and materials that you'll love.

By choosing Skriuwer, you're also supporting **Frisian**—a minority language mainly spoken in the northern Netherlands. Although **Frisian** has a rich history, the number of speakers is shrinking, and it's at risk of dying out. Your purchase helps fund resources to preserve and promote this language, such as educational programs and learning tools. If you'd like to learn more about Frisian or even start learning it yourself, please visit **www.learnfrisian.com**.

Thank you for being part of our community. We look forward to sharing more books with you in the future.

**Warm regards,**
The Skriuwer Team

www.ingramcontent.com/pod-product-compliance
Lightning Source LLC
LaVergne TN
LVHW012035070526
838202LV00056B/5508